FREE

Free Study Tips Videos/DVD

In addition to this guide, we have created a FREE set of videos with helpful study tips. **These FREE videos provide you with top-notch tips to conquer your exam and reach your goals.**

Our simple request is that you give us feedback about the book in exchange for these strategy-packed videos. We would love to hear what you thought about the book, whether positive, negative, or neutral. It is our #1 goal to provide you with quality products and customer service.

To receive your **FREE Study Tips Videos**, scan the QR code or email freevideos@apexprep.com. Please put "FREE Videos" in the subject line and include the following in the email:

   a. The title of the book

   b. Your rating of the book on a scale of 1-5, with 5 being the highest score

   c. Any thoughts or feedback about the book

Thank you!

CDL Study Guide 2022-2023
CDL Manual for Exam Prep & Practice Test Questions Book
[Includes Detailed Answer Explanations]

J. M. Lefort

Copyright © 2022 by APEX Publishing

All rights reserved. This book or any portion thereof may not be reproduced or used in any manner whatsoever without the express written permission of the publisher except for the use of brief quotations in a book review.

Written and edited by APEX Publishing.

ISBN 13: 9781637752883
ISBN 10: 1637752881

APEX Publishing is not connected with or endorsed by any official testing organization. APEX Publishing creates and publishes unofficial educational products. All test and organization names are trademarks of their respective owners.

The material in this publication is included for utilitarian purposes only and does not constitute an endorsement by APEX Publishing of any particular point of view.

For additional information or for bulk orders, contact info@apexprep.com.

Table of Contents

Test Taking Strategies 1
FREE Videos/DVD OFFER 4
Introduction for the CDL Test 5
Study Prep Plan for the CDL Test 7
Driving Safely 9
   Practice Questions 30
   Answer Explanations 31
Transporting Cargo and Passengers Safely 32
   Practice Questions 37
   Answer Explanations 38
Air Brakes 39
   Practice Questions 44
   Answer Explanations 45
Combination Vehicles 46
   Practice Questions 65
   Answer Explanations 66
Doubles and Triples 67
   Practice Questions 73
   Answer Explanations 74
Tank Vehicles 75
   Practice Questions 79
   Answer Explanations 80
Hazardous Materials 81
   Practice Questions 103
   Answer Explanations 104
School Buses 105
   Practice Questions 114
   Answer Explanations 115
Pre-Trip Vehicle Inspection Test 116
   Practice Questions 126
   Answer Explanations 127

Basic Vehicle Control Skills Test 128
Practice Questions 130
Answer Explanations 131
On-Road Driving 132
Practice Test 135
Answer Explanations 148

Test Taking Strategies

1. Reading the Whole Question

A popular assumption in Western culture is the idea that we don't have enough time for anything. We speed while driving to work, we want to read an assignment for class as quickly as possible, or we want the line in the supermarket to dwindle faster. However, speeding through such events robs us from being able to thoroughly appreciate and understand what's happening around us. While taking a timed test, the feeling one might have while reading a question is to find the correct answer as quickly as possible. Although pace is important, don't let it deter you from reading the whole question. Test writers know how to subtly change a test question toward the end in various ways, such as adding a negative or changing focus. If the question has a passage, carefully read the whole passage as well before moving on to the questions. This will help you process the information in the passage rather than worrying about the questions you've just read and where to find them. A thorough understanding of the passage or question is an important way for test takers to be able to succeed on an exam.

2. Examining Every Answer Choice

Let's say we're at the market buying apples. The first apple we see on top of the heap may *look* like the best apple, but if we turn it over we can see bruising on the skin. We must examine several apples before deciding which apple is the best. Finding the correct answer choice is like finding the best apple. Although it's tempting to choose an answer that seems correct at first without reading the others, it's important to read each answer choice thoroughly before making a final decision on the answer. The aim of a test writer might be to get as close as possible to the correct answer, so watch out for subtle words that may indicate an answer is incorrect. Once the correct answer choice is selected, read the question again and the answer in response to make sure all your bases are covered.

3. Eliminating Wrong Answer Choices

Sometimes we become paralyzed when we are confronted with too many choices. Which frozen yogurt flavor is the tastiest? Which pair of shoes look the best with this outfit? What type of car will fill my needs as a consumer? If you are unsure of which answer would be the best to choose, it may help to use process of elimination. We use "filtering" all the time on sites such as eBay® or Craigslist® to eliminate the ads that are not right for us. We can do the same thing on an exam. Process of elimination is crossing out the answer choices we know for sure are wrong and leaving the ones that might be correct. It may help to cover up the incorrect answer choice. Covering incorrect choices is a psychological act that alleviates stress due to the brain being exposed to a smaller amount of information. Choosing between two answer choices is much easier than choosing between all of them, and you have a better chance of selecting the correct answer if you have less to focus on.

4. Sticking to the World of the Question

When we are attempting to answer questions, our minds will often wander away from the question and what it is asking. We begin to see answer choices that are true in the real world instead of true in the world of the question. It may be helpful to think of each test question as its own little world. This world may be different from ours. This world may know as a truth that the chicken came before the egg or may assert that two plus two equals five. Remember that, no matter what hypothetical nonsense may be in the question, assume it to be true. If the question states that the chicken came before the egg, then choose

Test Taking Strategies

your answer based on that truth. Sticking to the world of the question means placing all of our biases and assumptions aside and relying on the question to guide us to the correct answer. If we are simply looking for answers that are correct based on our own judgment, then we may choose incorrectly. Remember an answer that is true does not necessarily answer the question.

5. Key Words

If you come across a complex test question that you have to read over and over again, try pulling out some key words from the question in order to understand what exactly it is asking. Key words may be words that surround the question, such as *main idea, analogous, parallel, resembles, structured,* or *defines*. The question may be asking for the main idea, or it may be asking you to define something. Deconstructing the sentence may also be helpful in making the question simpler before trying to answer it. This means taking the sentence apart and obtaining meaning in pieces, or separating the question from the foundation of the question. For example, let's look at this question:

> Given the author's description of the content of paleontology in the first paragraph, which of the following is most parallel to what it taught?

The question asks which one of the answers most *parallels* the following information: The *description* of paleontology in the first paragraph. The first step would be to see *how* paleontology is described in the first paragraph. Then, we would find an answer choice that parallels that description. The question seems complex at first, but after we deconstruct it, the answer becomes much more attainable.

6. Subtle Negatives

Negative words in question stems will be words such as *not, but, neither,* or *except*. Test writers often use these words in order to trick unsuspecting test takers into selecting the wrong answer—or, at least, to test their reading comprehension of the question. Many exams will feature the negative words in all caps (*which of the following is NOT an example*), but some questions will add the negative word seamlessly into the sentence. The following is an example of a subtle negative used in a question stem:

> According to the passage, which of the following is *not* considered to be an example of paleontology?

If we rush through the exam, we might skip that tiny word, *not*, inside the question, and choose an answer that is opposite of the correct choice. Again, it's important to read the question fully, and double check for any words that may negate the statement in any way.

7. Spotting the Hedges

The word "hedging" refers to language that remains vague or avoids absolute terminology. Absolute terminology consists of words like *always, never, all, every, just, only, none,* and *must*. Hedging refers to words like *seem, tend, might, most, some, sometimes, perhaps, possibly, probability,* and *often*. In some cases, we want to choose answer choices that use hedging and avoid answer choices that use absolute terminology. It's important to pay attention to what subject you are on and adjust your response accordingly.

8. Restating to Understand

Every now and then we come across questions that we don't understand. The language may be too complex, or the question is structured in a way that is meant to confuse the test taker. When you come across a question like this, it may be worth your time to rewrite or restate the question in your own words in order to understand it better. For example, let's look at the following complicated question:

> Which of the following words, if substituted for the word *parochial* in the first paragraph, would LEAST change the meaning of the sentence?

Let's restate the question in order to understand it better. We know that they want the word *parochial* replaced. We also know that this new word would "least" or "not" change the meaning of the sentence. Now let's try the sentence again:

> Which word could we replace with *parochial,* and it would not change the meaning?

Restating it this way, we see that the question is asking for a synonym. Now, let's restate the question so we can answer it better:

> Which word is a synonym for the word *parochial*?

Before we even look at the answer choices, we have a simpler, restated version of a complicated question.

9. Predicting the Answer

After you read the question, try predicting the answer *before* reading the answer choices. By formulating an answer in your mind, you will be less likely to be distracted by any wrong answer choices. Using predictions will also help you feel more confident in the answer choice you select. Once you've chosen your answer, go back and reread the question and answer choices to make sure you have the best fit. If you have no idea what the answer may be for a particular question, forego using this strategy.

10. Avoiding Patterns

One popular myth in grade school relating to standardized testing is that test writers will often put multiple-choice answers in patterns. A runoff example of this kind of thinking is that the most common answer choice is "C," with "B" following close behind. Or, some will advocate certain made-up word patterns that simply do not exist. Test writers do not arrange their correct answer choices in any kind of pattern; their choices are randomized. There may even be times where the correct answer choice will be the same letter for two or three questions in a row, but we have no way of knowing when or if this might happen. Instead of trying to figure out what choice the test writer probably set as being correct, focus on what the *best answer choice* would be out of the answers you are presented with. Use the tips above, general knowledge, and reading comprehension skills in order to best answer the question, rather than looking for patterns that do not exist.

FREE Videos/DVD OFFER

Achieving a high score on your exam depends on both understanding the content and applying your knowledge. **Because your success is our primary goal, we offer FREE Study Tips Videos, which provide top-notch test taking strategies to help optimize your testing experience.**

Our simple request is that you email us feedback about our book in exchange for the strategy-packed videos.

To receive your **FREE Study Tips Videos**, scan the QR code or email freevideos@apexprep.com. Please put "FREE Videos" in the subject line and include the following in the email:

   a. The title of the book

   b. Your rating of the book on a scale of 1-5, with 5 being the highest score

   c. Any thoughts or feedback about the book

Thank you!

Introduction for the CDL Test

Function of the Test

To drive a Commercial Motor Vehicle (CMV), it is necessary to obtain a Commercial Driver's License (CDL). There are many types of CMVs, including semi-trucks, combination vehicles, tankers, and school buses.

CDLs are issued by state government agencies (usually called the Department of Motor Vehicles, Department of Transportation, or something similar), and drivers must obtain their CDL from their state of residence. Because the CDL requirements are established by the state, they may vary based on location. Before participating in any testing, all potential drivers are advised to obtain a copy of their state's CDL manual, which provides state-specific requirements for licensure.

Some vehicles will require a special endorsement in addition to the standard CDL. These may include vehicles transporting passengers or hazardous materials, vehicles with double or triple trailers, or tank vehicles. Obtaining these endorsements may require additional written and/or on-road testing.

Test Administration

Potential drivers must schedule an appointment with their local state agency to take the written test first. There may be other requirements at this time, such as a vision test. Check your state agency's website to identify the necessary paperwork, which may include identify verification documents, insurance documents, and medical status certification.

After passing the written test, applicants receive a commercial learner's permit, which they must possess for a certain period of time (e.g., 14 days) before scheduling the skills test. Once in possession of the permit, they may practice driving a CMV with another driver who has an active CDL. When ready to take the skills test, applicants must once again make an appointment with the state agency. Drivers are required to provide their own vehicle in which to take the skills test.

Test Format

To obtain their CDL, new drivers will have to take at least one written knowledge test. Knowledge tests examine drivers' understanding of general concepts, air brakes, passenger safety, hazardous materials, and more. Depending on the type of CMV, drivers will also be tested on their knowledge of transporting tanks, pulling multiple trailers, driving combination CMVs, and driving a school bus.

The specific format depends on the state administering the test. In most cases, there will be a written test covering general knowledge in multiple choice format as well as a skills test covering vehicle inspection, vehicle control (e.g., backing up, parallel parking, etc.), and on-road driving. There are additional tests for each type of special endorsement.

The on-road test involves putting the driver in a variety of environments, from traffic-heavy highways to rough roads. The test proctor needs to see that the driver is paying attention to the road, obeying traffic laws, and is safely operating the CMV in different road conditions, such as encountering curves, switching lanes, or making wide turns. Drivers will be asked to shift gears, use signals, and apply the brakes. They may also be asked to pull off the road and simulate an emergency situation.

Scoring

Scoring may vary based on state. Many states administer a 50-question general knowledge test and require a passing score of 80% or higher. Applicants who are pursuing specific endorsements will have to take additional written tests that will also vary in length. Contact your local agency for more information about their specific requirements.

Study Prep Plan for the CDL Test

① Breathe
Reducing stress is key when preparing for your test.

② Build
Create a study plan to help you stay on track.

③ Begin
Stick with your study plan. You've got this!

1 Week Study Plan

Day 1	Day 2	Day 3	Day 4	Day 5	Day 6	Day 7
Driving Safely	Transporting Cargo and Passengers Safely	Combination Vehicles	Tank Vehicles	School Buses	Practice Test	Take Your Exam!

2 Week Study Plan

Day 1	Day 2	Day 3	Day 4	Day 5	Day 6	Day 7
Driving Safely	Driving at Night	Transporting Cargo and Passengers Safely	Air Brakes	Combination Vehicles	Antilock Brake Systems	Doubles and Triples

Day 8	Day 9	Day 10	Day 11	Day 12	Day 13	Day 14
Hazardous Materials	Driving and Parking Rules	School Buses	Pre-Trip Vehicle Inspection Test	Basic Vehicle Control Skills Test	Practice Test	Take Your Exam!

Study Prep Plan for the CDL Test

30 Day Study Plan

Day 1	Day 2	Day 3	Day 4	Day 5	Day 6	Day 7
Driving Safely	Managing Space	Mountain Driving	Practice Questions	Transporting Cargo and Passengers Safely	Practice Questions	Air Brakes

Day 8	Day 9	Day 10	Day 11	Day 12	Day 13	Day 14
Practice Questions	Combination Vehicles	Combination Vehicle Air Brakes	Coupling and Uncoupling	Practice Questions	Doubles and Triples	Practice Questions

Day 15	Day 16	Day 17	Day 18	Day 19	Day 20	Day 21
Tank Vehicles	Practice Questions	Hazardous Materials	Loading and Unloading	Emergencies	Practice Questions	School Buses

Day 22	Day 23	Day 24	Day 25	Day 26	Day 27	Day 28
Practice Questions	Pre-Trip Vehicle Inspection Test	Practice Questions	Basic Vehicle Control Skills Test	Practice Questions	On-Road Driving	Practice Test

Day 29	Day 30
Answer Explanations	Take Your Exam!

Driving Safely

Inspection of Vehicle

In order to obtain a commercial driver's license (CDL), you will be subject to several tests, one of which is vehicle inspection. During the vehicle inspection portion, potential drivers must prove that they understand which parts of a commercial motor vehicle (CMV) need to be checked prior to getting on the road.

The inspection involves a general walk around the CMV and identification/explanation of every part that needs to be inspected. Parts of the vehicle that should be inspected include:

- Horn
- Tires and wheels/rims
- Steering wheel
- Brakes and brake lights
- Suspension
- Exhaust system
- Turn signals
- Flashers
- Wipers
- Hoses
- Belts
- Gear shifts

These are just some parts of the CMV that must be checked while testing. You will also need to look for other things that could be hazardous to the driver or passengers, such as protruding wires, leaking oil or other fluids, and whether the vehicle is leaning. You must also check wheel alignment. The inspection is usually broken down into two parts: internal and external.

Internal Inspection

Inspection of internal parts begins by looking for signs of issues; look for puddles and dripping liquids, then inspect the water pump and alternator. Make sure that the power steering fluid, brake fluid, coolant, and oil are all at the right levels. The air compressor should not have any leaks and should be secured. The engine must start safely with all gears moving smoothly. The air, temperature, and oil pressure gauges must all be working properly; the air gauge must be able to build to 120-140 psi.

The horn must work. The ammeter/voltmeter must show that the alternator and/or generator is charging; the warning light should not be on. All lights (front, rear, etc.) must shine brightly and be free of cracks or debris. All mirrors and windshields must be properly adjusted, clean, and free of cracks or debris. The parking, hydraulic, air, and service brakes must all be secure and functional; you will be asked either to pump or maneuver them. The safety belt must be intact and secured correctly.

Finally, there should be a complete emergency kit with the correct emergency numbers, tire chains and other applicable equipment, spare fuses and flares, and a fire extinguisher.

External Inspection

An external inspection of a CMV includes several elements. The steering box, hoses, and linkage should be intact, have no leaks, and include all parts (nuts, bolts, etc.). All parts of the brakes should be without

Driving Safely

leaks. The proper brake linings should be visible; drums, discs, and hoses should lack wear and tear; and adjustors, pushrods, and chambers should be free of cracks and mounted securely. You should also be able to pull and release the brakes or shift them into each gear without issue.

Tires should be properly inflated; their tread depth should be 4/32 of an inch (steering) and 2/32 of an inch (remaining tires), and they should be in fair, equal condition. Grease and axle seals must have enough oil and no leaks. Rims must not be scratched, rusted, or loose. Shock absorbers should not have any leaks and should be secured in place. Mounts must not be damaged in any way.

There should be no leaks in the fuel tank, and the gas cap must be closed tightly. The exhaust system must not have any rust or leaks, and it must not exhibit any other signs of damage. Side marker lights and reflectors must be functional and clearly visible. High beams, emergency lights, four-way flashers, and all other lights must work; there must be no debris or visible damage on any of these lights. The catwalk or stairs must be tightly fastened to the truck; they must be able to extend as intended and hold steady in place.

Door hinges and mirror brackets must be firmly attached to the vehicle, and you must be able to maneuver or open them in appropriate directions. Indicator lights (oil, circuit, brakes) should not stay on if they light up when the vehicle is turned on. Heating and defrosting should work properly. Wipers must be able to move correctly, and they must not exhibit any wear and tear. The clutch, transmission controls, and accelerator must not "stick" or jam in any way.

There must be an emergency exit that is not blocked or jammed. Seat frames must be securely bolted yet adjustable, able to move forward and back. Ensure that the skid plate is hitched correctly to the CMV and is not missing any bolts; it must be supported by a platform structure (fifth wheel).

Basic Control of Your Vehicle

Basic control tests are usually performed in safe, secluded areas like a back street, an empty lot away from other drivers, or off-road. The skills assessed include steering, accelerating, backing up, parking, and stopping. The ability to back up safely is given slightly more attention because it requires a specific amount of skill, and there are several ways to maneuver while backing up.

Don't forget to fasten your safety belt! Read on to find out which areas are of particular importance to examiners.

Steering
You must have a firm grip on the steering wheel at the 10:00 and 2:00 positions. Driving with one hand is not permitted (nor is it safe!), and the examiner will dock points if you use this position while completing the basic skills portion of the test. Holding the wheel firmly will help if you encounter rough roads, especially those with potholes.

Accelerating
Drivers are assessed on how smoothly and gradually they accelerate while following designated and legal speeds. Roughly accelerating or pushing one's foot down too quickly and forcefully can result in loss of control or other accidents. If operating under harsh weather conditions like rain or snow, drivers must be able to accelerate or slow down safely.

Stopping

Stopping needs to be done as carefully and gradually as accelerating. Drivers must be able to push down the brake and/or clutch to come to a gradual stop that is appropriate for the speed at which they were driving. Do not slam on the brakes!

Parking

CMV drivers are advised to park only in "pull through" spaces. You must be able to pull straight through the space instead of backing out of it. Observe how the parking lot is set up and determine the best entrance and exit for the vehicle.

Drivers may also be asked to parallel park both from the passenger's and driver's sides. Examiners may set up a specific area marked by cones. The best technique for parallel parking is driving up next to the space, pulling ahead of it, and then slowly backing into it, carefully turning the wheel and watching the correct mirrors.

Backing Up

The CMV should be parked in a way that enables the driver to pull out safely. Before pulling out, the driver must make sure their path is clear. Look around the vehicle before getting inside it. Make sure the CMV has proper clearance overhead and on the sides.

Once inside, check all mirrors. If they aren't straight or you can't see in them clearly, adjust them. As noted previously, the mirrors should be clean, and there shouldn't be any smudges or other items that could obstruct the view. Look to make sure that nothing is in the way outside, especially people and other vehicles.

Put the vehicle in the lowest reverse gear and back up slowly, turning toward the driver's side. This is the safest way to back up, and it provides the best view for watching the vehicle's end and side while backing up.

Large vehicles like CMVs infamously have terrible blind spots, so asking for assistance when backing up is recommended. Establish appropriate hand signals that the driver and assistant understand.

If there is a trailer hitched to the CMV, the driver must back up differently. Whether backing up from the driver's or passenger's side, try to make the trailer as straight as you can. The examiner will be observing to make sure that you are using mirrors, backing up at a safe speed, steering in the right direction, and repositioning the vehicle as needed.

Shifting Gears

Using the correct gears while operating a CMV is optimal for precise control. If a CMV has a synchronized manual transmission, the driver will not have to double clutch as they would with unsynchronized versions. Shifting up requires a few specific steps:

1. Simultaneously push the clutch, shift to neutral, and release the accelerator.
2. Release the clutch.
3. Allow the gears and the engine to slow down to the appropriate revolutions per minute (RPMs).
4. Simultaneously shift to a higher gear and push the clutch.
5. At the same time, push the accelerator and let go of the clutch.

Do all of this gently; do not be too forceful. It will take time to master shifting up correctly. It is also important to know exactly when to shift up. This can be determined using road speed or engine speed.

Road speed is measured in miles per hour (mph). Drivers must learn which speeds and gears correspond best. Typically, it is suggested to change gears in 15 mph increments. So, shift to first gear at 15 mph, then to second gear at 30 mph, and so on.

Engine speed is measured in RPMs. The CMV should come with a driver's manual that provides specific ranges for each gear shift. It is recommended that drivers shift up when their tachometers meet the highest point of each range.

Just like shifting up, shifting down comes with a unique set of instructions:

1. Simultaneously move to neutral, apply pressure to the clutch, and release the accelerator.
2. Release the clutch.
3. Accelerate and increase the engine and gear speed to the recommended level.
4. Simultaneously shift to a lower gear and apply pressure to the clutch.
5. Finally, push the accelerator and let go of the clutch at the same time.

As with shifting up, the driver can either use RPM or mph to determine when to shift down. Always downshift when driving around curvy roads or traveling downhill. In these situations, you must slow down and apply light pressure to the brakes to stabilize the vehicle.

There are a few other systems to consider when operating a CMV. See if the vehicle has retarders. Retarders are devices that help slow a vehicle down (using the drive wheels), eliminating the need for excessive braking. The driver has the option of turning these devices on or leaving them off. If they are turned on, the best way to activate them is to stop pushing the accelerator.

If a driver decides that they need extra gears while driving, they can turn on the multi-speed rear axles and auxiliary transmissions. Because there are several different shift patterns when using these additions, drivers should refer to their vehicle's manual for guidance.

Automatic transmissions also help with braking. Transmissions are typically 10-speed transmissions, and not all vehicles have them. It's best to use them when shifting down gear levels.

Seeing

No driver can safely operate a vehicle without observing their surroundings. To start with, they need to look far enough beyond their vehicle. Drivers need to see how much room they have to accelerate, turn, back up, and complete other maneuvers while driving a CMV so they do not cause accidents.

Generally, it is recommended that drivers look ahead 12 to 15 seconds. This will vary based on how fast they are driving, of course. Drivers need to do this *and* be aware of the distance immediately in front of and around them.

Being aware of surrounding vehicles is incredibly important when driving a CMV, just as it is when driving a standard-sized car. The driver needs to be alert and keep a safe distance from other vehicles that are braking, merging, making turns, or coming to a complete stop. If another vehicle is trying to pass them, a CMV driver should neither accelerate nor slow down to prevent or enable them to pass; they need to keep driving at the same speed. Accelerating or slowing down abruptly endangers everyone on the road.

Driving Safely

On the other hand, if the driver encounters another vehicle that is being driven erratically, they must figure out how to get out of the way safely. They should not make any quick moves, like switching lanes, unless the road is clear.

Roads have twists and turns that drivers need to look out for. Looking in the wrong direction while driving around a curve could prove to be fatal. It is also important for drivers to follow all legal speeds and traffic signs.

Look out for roadwork signs and construction workers. It is essential to look out for signs that specify where vehicles of a certain size cannot pass.

Be aware of activity to the sides and rear of the CMV. Adjust mirrors before getting on the road, and frequently check them while driving. The best view occurs when a truck's trailer is straight. Watch vehicles behind and to the sides of the truck in case you need to change lanes, stop, or turn.

CDL drivers should be aware of their vehicle's blind spots. The mirrors on the CMV may not show everything. Being alert and aware of surrounding vehicles is the best way to avoid collisions. If you need to switch lanes, make sure the lane to which you intend to switch is clear and that any vehicles behind you are at a safe distance.

Make sure that there is nothing out of place on the vehicle. Chains, straps, or tarps can come loose; if any of these issues are observed, pull over when it is safe to do so and fix them.

Keep an eye on all cargo to ensure that nothing is moving around too freely. Regularly look at the tires in the mirrors in case any irregularities occur like a burst tire or fire and smoke.

Never lose focus of the road! A CMV is a more dangerous vehicle to handle than the average car. Just as you would keep alert of all surroundings while driving a car, you must watch the road, neighboring vehicles, and mirrors when driving a CMV.

Drivers should have their vision checked by optometrists on an annual basis to determine if they have any vision problems. They may be prescribed glasses or contact lenses to help them see. If this is the case, drivers need to wear these items as prescribed, especially if they're recommended for night vision. Note that it is illegal for anyone with their prescription for corrective lenses on their license to drive without them. It's also a good idea to keep a spare pair of glasses or extra contacts handy when on the road.

Communicating

Always use the proper signals before switching lanes, merging, or turning; do not wait until the last minute to turn on your signal! This is especially important when making a tight turn. Other drivers need to be alerted of your intent to turn several yards in advance. Do not turn if there is any chance that the truck's trailer could hit another vehicle in the process.

Do not speed while making sudden maneuvers. Always turn on the signal light. Once the turn, merge, or lane change is complete, make sure the signal is off. If the signal is left on, it could make other drivers think that you are planning to turn or change lanes when you are not. This can be a safety hazard, not to mention that it's incredibly annoying to follow behind a driver who has forgotten that their signal is on!

Before stopping, warn drivers behind you by tapping on the brake lights. If driving a long distance at a slow speed, turn on the emergency flashers. These hazard lights should also be used if there is an accident or another issue ahead, like a roadblock; this is a courtesy for the drivers behind you who may not be able

to see what's happening. In addition, hazard lights should be used when pulling over to park. Tapping the brakes may not be enough to get the attention of other drivers. The legal use of emergency or hazard lights varies from state to state. Please check your state's commercial vehicle driving manual.

Do not give other drivers "instructions" while driving, such as flashing your lights behind someone who is driving too slowly. Actions like this could alarm them and cause serious accidents.

Use low-beam headlights in low lighting, like daybreak or inclement weather such as pouring rain. This enables other drivers to see your vehicle from a distance.

Emergency warning devices must be placed around the CMV within minutes if a driver must make an emergency stop on the side of a highway. These devices must be placed 200, 100, and 10 feet behind the vehicle to warn oncoming traffic. If you are stopped along a two-lane road, place the devices at the front and rear of the vehicle at 10 and 100 feet. If stopped along a curve, place the devices within 100 and 500 feet of the rear of the vehicle.

Many drivers struggle to decide when it is appropriate to use their horn. Never use it out of anger or frustration at another driver. People driving smaller vehicles can be easily startled by the blaring horn of a commercial vehicle. Instead, get in the habit of only tapping the horn lightly to warn drivers when they are too close to the CMV, slide into the CMV's lane, or move suddenly in front of it as if they cannot see it. Of course, there are exceptions, such as when an accident occurs abruptly and you need to warn other drivers.

Controlling Speed

Drivers must be able to adjust and control their speed while driving a CMV according to the various speed limits, road conditions, curves, hills, and other conditions. Not driving at the right speed can result in serious accidents that cause injuries or death. Before getting behind the wheel, understand the relationship between speed and stopping distance.

The following equation determines stopping distance:

$$stopping\ distance\ = perception\ distance + reaction\ distance + braking\ distance + brake\ lag$$

Perception distance is the distance a vehicle travels from the time the driver sees a potential issue on the road to the time their brain recognizes it. Perception can be affected by other obstructions on the road, the driver's vision, overall visibility, and other factors. One and three-quarter seconds, or 142 feet at 55 mph, is a driver's average perception time.

The distance from when the driver sees an issue to just before they hit the brakes is the reaction distance. On average, drivers react within ¾ or 1 second or 61 feet at 55 mph.

Braking distance, as its name indicates, accounts for the distance covered between when the driver hits the brakes and when the vehicle comes to a complete stop. The average distance is 216 feet at 55 mph.

Brake lag is the amount of time it takes the brakes to activate after being pushed.

The average total stopping distance is 419 feet at 55 mph. The total stopping distance is quadrupled when a driver doubles their speed, therefore increasing the chance of an accidents. If a driver triples their speed, their stopping distance increases by a factor of nine. Keep in mind that slower speeds allow for a shorter stopping distance.

The more a CMV weighs, the harder it is to stop when driving at unsafe speeds. Interestingly, trucks that are fully loaded are easier to stop than empty ones. Having a loaded vehicle activates the springs, shock absorbers, tires, and brakes. Trying to stop an empty CMV is more difficult; the stopping distance is greater because the vehicle has little absorption.

Drivers should never exceed the posted speed limit. Downgrading gears increases a vehicle's speed, so drivers must be careful which gears they choose. It is also important to maintain the proper speed when serious weather events occur to ensure proper driving distance.

Drivers must adjust their speeds according to road surfaces. A road wet with rain will have different traction than a rough, bumpy one. Snow, ice, hail, excessive dirt, rocks, and uneven pavement are all hazards that may require a driver to slow down or pull over until conditions improve.

It takes longer to stop on a hazardous road, so it is important to stop slowly with the total stopping distance equation in mind. Total stopping distance is often doubled or tripled on wet roads. To determine whether a road is slippery and/or hazardous, look for the following things:

- Melting ice
- Black ice
- Bridges (especially in cold weather)
- Shaded areas of road
- Vehicle has icy/frozen windows and mirrors
- Rain
- Slush

Some hazards are unavoidable. The following are the most common road conditions that CMV drivers encounter.

Hydroplaning. Hydroplaning occurs when a vehicle encounters so much water on the road that it makes the tire lose contact with the pavement, causing the vehicle to slide back and forth out of the driver's control. Hydroplaning can happen in very little water or slush on the road. It's not possible to fully prepare for it, but drivers should ensure that their CMV's tire pressure and tread are in good shape before driving.

When the driver of a large truck hydroplanes, the first thing they need to do is stop accelerating. The second thing they need to do is avoid immediately hitting the brakes. Accelerating and braking too quickly cause vehicles to skid, endangering everyone in the surrounding area, especially the driver. Instead, the driver should push the clutch, which will cause the truck to slow down without the need to hit the brakes.

Curves. Drivers should remember two things when approaching curves: never brake and never speed. Braking through a curve can increase the risk of skidding. Instead, drivers should slow down as they approach the curve. Speeding can send a truck on a collision course off the side of the road, or the truck could completely flip over. Drivers should approach curves slowly and avoid going over the speed limit. If a curve is uphill, it is okay to accelerate a small amount in an appropriate gear to prevent the CMV from rolling backward.

Traffic. Traffic is the bane of many drivers' existence. It is miserable to be stuck in a seemingly endless number of cars moving at a turtle's pace or not moving at all. Although some drivers illegally drive on the sides of the traffic lanes to bypass everyone who is stuck, we strongly advise CMV drivers against that.

The best thing for CMV drivers to do is keep a safe distance between their vehicles and other cars. They also need to travel at the same speed as the surrounding traffic. It's best to just be patient and wait it out.

Managing Space

Commercial vehicles take up a lot of space, and it is important for CDL drivers to learn how to manage that space. Quick maneuvers and thinking on the road mean nothing if the driver doesn't have enough space to operate their vehicle.

Never follow another vehicle too closely, especially if it is smaller than the one you're driving. Most accidents between CMVs and other cars occur because there was not enough space between the vehicles. Most often, the cars in front of CMVs hit their brakes abruptly, leaving little time for the CMV driver to push their own brakes, causing them to slam into the other car. Remember to consider stopping distance to ensure there is the right amount of distance between your truck and the vehicle in front of it.

Drivers can estimate how much space is between their vehicle and the one ahead by counting after the vehicle in front has passed a mile-marker, landmark, tree, or other identifier. They should count the number of seconds it takes them to pass the same marker. It's important for drivers to know the length of their own trucks when making this calculation. They're driving too closely if it only takes them a couple of seconds to reach the marker, especially if they're driving a 60-foot truck at 50 mph.

Road conditions also factor into how closely vehicles should follow each other. More space should be allotted if there is inclement weather to allow room for overcorrection and to help avoid sudden accidents.

It's incredibly common for other vehicles to tailgate CMVs. Because CMVs are so large, it can be difficult for drivers to see if there's anything directly behind them on the road. Drivers of small cars are especially troublesome because the CMV drivers ahead of them most likely will not see them in their rearview mirrors.

If you discover that you are being followed too closely, don't increase your speed. Doing so may just encourage the other driver to speed up unnecessarily and continue tailgating. Don't suddenly tap the brakes to flash the brake lights or quickly change lanes either. There's no way to know how the driver behind will react. The safest thing to do is allow the driver to pass if they decide to. There should be enough space in front of your vehicle to enable this.

Always drive in the center of the lane; driving too closely to the right or left could take up too much space and endanger drivers in other lanes. You could also end up careening off the road if you make a sudden turn or go around a curve.

Try to avoid driving alongside other vehicles in windy conditions. Although a CMV is heavier and less likely to be moved by these winds, small cars often aren't as lucky and could blow into the CMV. The best option might be to pull over and wait out the windstorm.

Do your best to keep a safe distance between your truck and other vehicles. Changing lanes when driving can also be dangerous. If the lane next to you is clear and you need to merge into it, make sure there is enough space in front of and behind your truck before you move.

Overhead space is incredibly important. The allowed height posted on bridges and other infrastructure isn't always correct. If a driver isn't confident that their vehicle will fit, they should travel on an alternative route. Weight is significant when it comes to CMV height. The heights of heavily loaded vehicles are often

Driving Safely

lower due to the weight of the cargo, while unloaded vehicles might be taller. Take this into consideration when driving under overpasses. Approach all overpasses slowly in case your vehicle is too tall for the clearance. When backing up, look out for items that could scrape against the top of CMV, such as hanging wires.

Don't forget about the space below your vehicle, which can be limited. Bumpy roads, railroad tracks, debris in the roadway, and other hazards pose threats to the bottom of your CMV. These items can get caught underneath, or the truck itself can get stuck.

Finally, drivers need to monitor their truck's space when entering traffic, changing lanes, or making turns. Drivers need to make sure that they have enough space to enter oncoming traffic before doing so. Even if you must wait a bit for a clear opening, that's much safer than obliviously diving into oncoming traffic, forcing other drivers to move.

When making turns, make sure that there is enough room so the trailer of your CMV doesn't hit other cars. If there is a risk of this happening, do not force the turn anyway. You may just need to reroute or come back to the turn when possible. When able to turn, do so slowly, and do not yank the wheel suddenly to the left or right.

Many CMVs must swing into another lane when turning. When turning from the left or right, turn wide to prevent other drivers from speeding past and crashing into the CMV. When you must cross an oncoming lane to make a turn, wait until it is clear and all oncoming cars have driven by.

Seeing Hazards

Potential dangers on the roadway are known as hazards. A driver cutting off another in traffic is a hazard, as is a pothole on the road. Being able to spot hazards is critical when driving massive vehicles. The sooner a driver spots a hazard, the more time they have to avoid an accident and get out of the way when possible. It also gives them time to alert other drivers to the danger, either by flashing their lights or signaling.

Pedestrians, cyclists, and children playing on the side of the road are all dangerous for drivers. Pedestrians sometimes cross streets that don't have pedestrian signals that tell them when to stop and go. Even if there are pedestrian signals, people will sometimes ignore them and cross when they deem it to be safe. Not every road will have a bike lane, especially back roads or highways. Ask any driver you know, and they can probably tell you of a time that they felt a cyclist was too close to their vehicle for comfort. Perhaps they had to move over a significant amount in their lane to avoid a collision with the cyclist. The potential for the person on the bike to topple over into the street, take a turn without using hand signals, or glide into a traffic lane is high. There may also be times when CMV drivers must go through residential neighborhoods. There could be children playing in their driveways or on the sides of the road near their homes. Children could run into the road chasing after a pet or a toy.

Construction and emergency workers are also potential hazards. It's easy to be distracted by construction work or an ambulance at the scene of an accident. Drivers have a natural tendency to slow down and look at such things—a habit also known as rubbernecking—which causes traffic to slow down. Drivers slowing down abruptly can cause a hazard.

By and large, other drivers are the most significant hazards of all. Talking, either on the phone or to other passengers, and texting while driving are examples of distracted driving. You may have been behind someone on the road who drifts in and out of lanes or drives erratically, and it turned out that they were on their phones. Intoxicated drivers exhibit similar driving patterns.

Tired or lost drivers can also cause problems. Someone falling in and out of sleep at the wheel threatens their life and the lives around them. They may weave in and out of traffic, stop suddenly, or run off the road. Similarly, someone who is lost might take their eyes off the road to stare at landmarks, a map, or GPS; they may start to careen into other lanes, stop abruptly, or even run off the road.

Other truck drivers can also be dangerous. Not everyone is a good driver; some may be driving a large truck for the first time. They may completely disregard road rules; their vehicles may become disabled, forcing them to pull off unsafely; or they might be distracted.

Bad weather is also a hazard. Ice, sleet, torrential rain, heavy snow, and strong winds are all dangerous and can cause fatalities.

Some other hazards you might encounter include:

- Window glare
- A driver using high beams
- A vehicle with nonfunctioning lights (taillights, headlights, etc.)
- Dirty mirrors and windows
- Unfinished roadwork

Pay attention to the road and your surroundings. The first step to avoiding the danger of hazards is the awareness that they can pop up anywhere and everywhere. Get into the habit of expecting to see hazards while driving and come up with a game plan for how to avoid the most common ones.

Distracted Driving

Distracted drivers risk their own lives and the lives of their passengers, other drivers, and innocent bystanders. According to the National Highway Traffic Safety Administration (NHTSA), 3,142 people died as a result of distracted driving in 2019. In addition, the NHTSA reported that more than 424,000 people were injured in accidents caused by distracted drivers.

Taking your eyes off the road for just a second is all it takes to crash your vehicle. Activities like texting, talking on a dispatching device, changing the radio station, adjusting the mirrors, and reaching for food and drink are all distractions. People often think it's safe to talk on the phone using Bluetooth or giving voice commands, but the truth is that these activities take drivers' attention away from the road just as much as if they were holding the phone up to their ear.

External distractions include looking at pedestrians, billboards, or unique cars on the road. According to the Federal Motor Carrier Safety Administration, 11,000 CMV accidents resulted from drivers being distracted by external factors.

CMV drivers are prohibited from using hand-held mobile devices while on the road. Being caught doing so can result in fines, conviction, or loss of the CDL. Exactly how many offenses it takes to remove a driver's CDL varies from state to state. Depending on the state, drivers may be permitted to use a hand-held electronic device to alert the authorities if an emergency arises. Check your state's commercial driving manual for specifics.

Driving Safely

Before departure, drivers should assess their CMVs for any potential internal distractions. They should also think of a few distraction scenarios that could happen while they're driving and how they would handle them. They can also take some precautionary measures such as ensuring that mirrors are correctly adjusted, preselecting the music they'd like to listen to, making sure any cargo is secured, starting their GPS, and turning off their cell phone. Grabbing a bite to eat and drink before leaving is also a good idea. If they do stop to grab some food on the way, they should park the vehicle and consume it before continuing their journey.

Drivers should also make sure they're in a good temperament before driving. Getting on the road after having an intense disagreement or receiving some disappointing news could lead them to be mentally distracted, which can be just as dangerous as physical distractions.

Studies have shown that brain activity increases when drivers are distracted and not solely focusing on driving. This increase in brain activity can impair a person's driving ability. Distracted driving and sleeping are two reasons that rumble road strips were invented; driving over these course lines on the road alerts the driver that they are running off the road.

Aggressive Drivers/Road Rage

According to the AAA Foundation for Traffic Safety, nearly half of all fatal vehicle accidents result from aggressive driving. Aggressive driving occurs when someone drives with disregard for the safety of others. One cause of aggressive driving is road rage, which can be influenced by increased traffic or behavior by one driver that angers another. The most common behavior involves an aggressive driver making lewd gestures, tailgating, screaming, and speeding in front of other drivers. In some instances, if both the aggressor and their target pull off the road, the aggressor may approach and/or attack their target.

If you encounter an aggressive driver, do not try to confront them, race them, or blow your horn at them. Move out of their way as best you can, do not look them in the eye, and do not gesture to or shout at them. If you can, switch lanes so that they can pass. If the aggressive driver is a danger to others, try to gather important details about their car, such as the license plate number (partial is fine), color of the car, and the make/model. Call the authorities and report what you have witnessed, providing these details. If you can, pull off when it is safe before making your call. If you witness an accident caused by an aggressive driver, pull over several feet from the crash site and wait for the police to arrive. If approached, tell the officers on the scene what you saw.

You can't change the behavior of an aggressive driver, but you can do your best not to be one. Before getting on the road, drivers should assess their attitudes. If they're having a bad day, driving in traffic will only make it worse. The best thing to do is try to calm down before getting behind the wheel.

Driving at Night

Many people have trouble seeing when driving at night. It's much harder to see issues on the road in the dark. Therefore, nighttime driving is less safe than daytime.

Sometimes, the blinding bright lights of another car make seeing at night even worse. Being unable to see because of someone's high beams can easily cause a driver to get in an accident or need to pull over. High beams from other cars can be blinding, but sometimes there are people who don't have their lights on at all! Make sure you are using the appropriate headlights so that you can see cars that don't have their lights on.

Being tired while driving is very dangerous. Drivers who are tired tend to zone out, making themselves and other drivers vulnerable. Their reaction time is slowed. And of course, the likelihood of their falling asleep puts everyone near them in grave danger. The NHTSA reported that nearly 700 people were killed in accidents involving sleepy drivers in 2019. To prevent drowsiness, drivers can do several things. The most obvious is to get an adequate amount of sleep. Exercising can also help energize someone before they drive. If possible, have another person ride along with you so that you can take turns driving. Caffeine can help, but it should be consumed in moderation to avoid "crashing," or coming down from the rush of caffeine. Cracking a window and allowing cool air to flow into the vehicle is another way to help keep drivers alert.

Streetlights along the highway are not always consistent. There might be great lighting that enables you to see everything in some areas, while others may not be as well lit. There is also such a thing as too much lighting, such as a street overrun with traffic signals, signs with lights on them, and shop lights. The combination of all these lights can be blinding for some drivers.

It's much harder to see pedestrians and cyclists at night. Not everyone who goes for a walk or a bike ride wears reflective clothing so that drivers can see them better.

You can never know what other drivers may do on the road, day or night. Nighttime is especially hazardous when there is an uptick in impaired drivers. Weaving in and out of a lane is a sign that someone might be intoxicated or falling asleep at the wheel.

Drivers should ensure that others can see them on the highway. Headlights should be clean and properly adjusted. Improperly situated headlights can distract drivers. High beams allow drivers to see up to 500 feet ahead of their vehicles, while low beams allow them to see half as much. When traveling on extremely dark roads, use high beams. If another car is more than 500 feet ahead of your vehicle, continue to use high beams. However, if they are any closer than that, switch to low beams. Get in the habit of switching to low beams when an oncoming vehicle is visible to avoid blinding the other driver.

The CMV should have reflectors in place. There should be clearance, marker, and identification lights. Both taillights need to work. Brake lights and turn signals also need to be operational.

It is always important to have clean windows and clean, properly adjusted mirrors. Dirty windows and mirrors create vision problems for drivers, including glare.

If you are too tired to drive, pull over somewhere safe. If need be, take a quick nap. Naps of 20 minutes or less can effectively rejuvenate people. If you still feel tired after taking a nap, find somewhere to turn in for the night. It's better to be a little behind schedule than risk your life.

Driving in Fog

Fog is a type of cloud. It happens when water vapor doesn't fully evaporate into the air, leaving it hanging above roadways. As the U.S. Department of Transportation reports, between 2007 and 2016, more than 25,000 vehicle crashes occurred due to fog. Over 400 of those crashes were fatal.

Driving in fog is incredibly dangerous. Fog can appear randomly, leaving the driver unprepared. It makes it very hard for a driver to see and safely operate a vehicle. If possible, pull off the road until the fog passes. Always check the weather forecast in advance so you can be prepared for various weather conditions.

Driving Safely

It is recommended that drivers not proceed in fog. They should not pull over to the shoulder or curve of a road, but in a space where they can leave some distance between their vehicle and the road. If they do pull over, they should turn on their hazard lights so other drivers can see them.

However, in some instances, drivers may not have a choice but to keep driving. In those instances, drivers should drive slowly and use their low-beam lights. Some trucks are equipped with fog lights that should be turned on when facing a foggy road. These lights alert other drivers to their presence and help drivers to see other vehicles that don't have their lights on.

Windshields can literally "fog up" too. If this happens, turn on the defrost to clear the windows and use windshield wipers if necessary.

CMV drivers should turn on their emergency flashers to further help other drivers see their vehicle. Some people may pull over to wait out the fog, so it's important to keep your eyes out for them. There might be roadside reflectors available to help safely guide you down the road.

Your following distance between other vehicles should increase by five additional seconds when driving in fog. Do not use cruise control. If you can't see the road well, crack your window and listen for other vehicles. If you do encounter another vehicle, do not pass or stop abruptly. There could also be a car in the fog that you cannot see. Being overly cautious can decrease collision risk.

Reduce the number of distractions in your vehicle. Turn down any music. Put your cell phone on silent or "Do Not Disturb," place it away from you, and do not reach for it while driving. Try to eliminate the need to eat while driving because that can be a distraction too.

Be on the lookout for animals, like deer, that may wander onto the highway during foggy conditions.

Black ice can form in foggy conditions when it is cold outside. The fog makes this ice nearly impossible to see, so drive slowly.

Winter Driving

Driving in the winter can be hazardous. Winter weather can pose a risk to CMV drivers. In addition to checking the weather before getting on the road, drivers should check their trucks for several things.

The first thing drivers should check is the antifreeze, or engine coolant, level. Antifreeze doesn't only keep the engine from freezing; it keeps it from overheating as well. A coolant tester, which can be purchased from hardware stores and other retailers, is used to check antifreeze levels.

Heaters and defrosters need to be in working order. In addition to the heating system that comes with the CMV, others such as mirror heaters can be purchased too. Drivers should understand how to operate the heaters and defrosters before driving.

It is important to have good windshield wipers and enough wiper fluid, especially in winter weather. Windshield washer fluid with antifreeze can be purchased at many hardware stores and should be used during the colder months. When windshield wipers show any signs of wear and tear, they should be replaced. They need to be the correct size and fit for the CMV in order to clear windshields effectively.

The tread of each tire should be checked. In order to drive through snow, ice, and other conditions, there needs to be a decent amount of tread on all tires: 4/32 inch on the front two tires and 2/32 inch tread on the rest. Drivers should keep a tire gauge handy to check tire tread periodically.

Drivers never know when they will come across mud or snow, so they should always carry chains and cross links. CMV trucks require specific chains, so it's important that drivers purchase the correct ones. In case the original cross links on the chains end up breaking, drivers should have extra ones available. The chains should not be rusted or damaged. Drivers need to practice applying the chains before leaving in order to know exactly how they fit.

Reflectors and lights must be operational and clean. Reflectors, specifically, need to be clearly visible to other drivers. Drivers should make sure all lights on the truck work and that all reflectors can be seen from a distance.

Inevitably, snow and ice will collect on windows and mirrors. Scrapers should always be handy to remove snow or ice. De-icer spray is also a helpful product that goes hand-in-hand with scrapers and defrosters. Before driving, remove any ice or snow from the mirrors and windows.

Most CMVs come with deck plates, hand holds, and steps. These three things can be covered in snow and ice, which could cause the driver to slip and fall. Be sure to clean them off regularly.

Winterfronts cover the grilles of trucks, protecting them from the elements. They need to be open just enough to avoid overheating. Radiator shutters allow air to flow to and from the truck's radiator. They need to be able to open, so they should be kept clean and free of ice and snow to prevent freezing.

Broken exhaust systems can leak carbon monoxide, which can be deadly for drivers. Exhaust systems must be checked regularly for leaks, cracks, loose parts, or other damage.

Driving in Very Hot Weather

When the weather is hot, CMV drivers should inspect the tires, engine oil, antifreeze, coolant hoses, and engine belts.

Hot tires are hazardous because they are in danger of blowing out or catching fire. These accidents are primarily caused by increased air pressure in the tires. Although this increase is temporary, tire air pressure needs to be monitored regularly when driving in the heat. Drivers should pull over every 100 miles and check the tire pressure. If the tires are extremely hot, it's best to remain parked until they cool down.

Drivers should always check the engine oil level and temperature. This oil helps cool down the engine, so its temperature should not exceed 220 °F. There should be between 10 and 15 gallons of oil in the engine, which is an adequate amount to keep it cool.

Antifreeze isn't only used in the winter. Engines have cooling systems that consist of 50 percent water and 50 percent antifreeze coolant. There should be enough of both to keep an engine between 195 °F and 220 °F. Engines that are too hot run the risk of catching fire. To figure out just how much oil and coolant the truck needs, the manufacturer's manual for the engine can be referenced. Most manufacturers provide downloadable manuals online. They can be found by searching the name and product number of the engine.

The engine and the coolant container should never be touched with bare hands. Touching these hot items can cause burns. After they have cooled off, a work glove can be used to open the coolant container for inspection. If water or antifreeze needs to be added, it should be done after the engine has fully cooled down. Neither these substances nor oil should be refilled while the engine is hot. To open a coolant container, apply pressure to its cap and then twist it to the right. To put it back on, apply pressure turn the cap to the left.

Coolant hoses should be in good, working condition. It is a fire hazard to have loose or broken hoses.

Engine belts need to be checked to make sure they aren't damaged or loose. Properly fitted belts help operate the engine fan and water pump.

While driving, look out for roads that are "bleeding" tar. Tar often seeps to the road surface during hot temperatures, and it can cause trucks to slip and slide around on the road.

Drivers should avoid speeding while driving in extreme heat. Driving too fast heats up the engine and tires, which could result in a fire. At the very least, it could overheat the engine and make it fail.

Railroad-Highway Crossings

When a railroad crosses a highway, it is called a level crossing. Drivers should be cautious when approaching this type of crossing. Even if warning signals are not displayed, a train could be coming. If a train is coming, a driver should not try to speed across the crossing because the train could be moving much faster than they think. The tires or wiring below the CMV could become stuck on the tracks. As soon as a driver sees a sign for a railway crossing, they should slow down. Failing to slow down fast enough could necessitate an abrupt stop, which could force the CMV to skid. It could also result in the truck sliding onto the train tracks.

If warning signals are displayed but the driver does not see or hear a train yet, that does not mean it's safe to cross. Some trains can't be heard until the last minute. Double train tracks are incredibly dangerous because more than one train can be coming from opposite directions. Drivers must not drive across the tracks unless the tracks are completely clear. Before crossing, they need to look to the left and right. The driver needs to make sure that there is no traffic on the opposite side of the tracks before driving over them. If the driver must change gears, it should be done before continuing to drive. If the road and railway are clear, they can proceed.

Mountain Driving

Drivers should look at road maps or GPS route details ahead of time to see if they will encounter any mountainous roads or other steep grades. Asking another driver who has gone the same route might help them prepare and figure out what to expect. All fluids and oil levels should be filled adequately before leaving for a drive around mountains. The engine should be checked, and the tank should be full of gas.

Driving on mountainous roads is hard. Drivers will have to shift gears accordingly when they go up or down mountains. Incorrect shifting can result in the truck rolling backward down a mountain or speeding down it too quickly. Lower gears should always be used when going down a mountain grade. If the driver is transporting a lot of cargo, this will affect their driving speed and ability to guide the truck. Being in too high of a gear while driving under these conditions could lead to a serious accident.

The driver should watch for and adhere to the recommended safe speed. Gears should be shifted carefully and as needed before proceeding up or down the mountain. The driver should observe cars in front of or behind them. If driving on a two-lane highway, the driver must be careful not to veer into the other lane. They should be aware of all surroundings, and they shouldn't take their eyes off the road. If driving at dusk or dawn, headlights need to be used.

If a driver knows they are going to drive on mountainous roads, they must check to make sure that the brakes are properly adjusted and all brake pads are in good shape. Worn out brake pads and improperly adjusted brakes regularly lead to brake failure. Braking too hard can overheat truck brakes, forcing them

Driving Safely

to give out or fade. Drivers should always brake slowly when going down a steep mountain grade. To brake properly, the following steps are recommended:

1. Apply the minimum amount of pressure to slow the truck.
2. Allow the speed to decrease by 5 mph under the recommended speed, then lift off the brakes.
3. Each time the speed increases again, repeat the first two steps.

If the safe speed is 50 mph, the driver should brake until they are going 45 mph while driving in the mountains.

Most mountain downgrades have escape ramps that are meant to catch vehicles when drivers lose control. The ramps are made from materials that will help to slow down and stop vehicles, like sand or gravel. Drivers should always veer over to the escape ramp if the brakes suddenly fail.

Driving Emergencies

CMV drivers should always be prepared for emergencies. Accidents, sudden weather changes, and empty fuel tanks are just a few things that drivers may face when going long distances. Mapping out gas stations along the way, packing a first aid kit, and having tire accessories, such as an air pump or chains, are all precautions drivers can take to prepare for their road trips. Sometimes a driver can have all the necessary supplies but still not feel prepared when an emergency occurs.

If a driver is behind another driver who has made a sudden stop on the highway, hitting the brakes should not be their first instinct. Instead, they should try to steer their CMV off the road or into another lane. Immeasurable damage could be caused by a CMV hitting a smaller vehicle or a similar truck. To make a quick turn off the road, drivers should follow these steps:

1. Do not hit the brakes. Doing so could cause the CMV to slide into another vehicle or flip off the road. Also, it's usually too late to brake in many emergency situations.

2. Turn the steering wheel slowly. Do not yank the steering wheel to get out of the way.

3. Once the truck is clear of the accident, counter-steer to straighten up the vehicle.

There is a reason CDL instructors usually tell new drivers to keep in the lane furthest to the right, especially on multilane highways. If an accident suddenly occurs or another vehicle violently swerves into the lane in front of them, the driver's best bet is to steer to the right and get off the road. Of course, this is not always possible; there could be a guard rail immediately to the right. The best thing drivers can do is keep watching their mirrors and surrounding traffic in anticipation of something like this happening. The safest place to steer will vary based on the situation.

When returning to the road, drivers need to use caution. When the lane is clear, they can proceed. If coming from the right of the road, they should turn sharply to the left until the two front tires of the CMV are on the pavement and then counter steer to the right to straighten the CMV and fully re-enter the lane.

If a driver is in a situation where they cannot pull off the road, they will likely need to stop. If a driver must stop during an emergency, they should use controlled braking or stab braking. Controlled braking is accomplished by using as much pressure as possible on the brakes and not locking the wheels. It involves a minimal amount of steering. If the wheels lock up, the driver needs to let go of the brakes for a few seconds before applying them again. With stab braking, the driver completely applies the brakes and releases them when the wheels lock. When the wheels begin to move again, this technique is repeated. To

Driving Safely

avoid skidding, drivers must not slam on the brakes. These two techniques involve a bit of finesse to brake safely.

Brake failure can be prevented. However, if the brakes fail in an emergency, there are some steps drivers should take. First, they should shift down into a lower gear, causing the CMV to slow down. Second, they should try pumping the brakes to create hydraulic pressure. Third, drivers should use the emergency brake and pull the release lever. Finally, they should look for an area to pull off the road. They should make sure this area is not uphill, is free of other vehicles, and is large enough to fit the CMV. The emergency brake should remain engaged while pulling off the road into this area. Ideally, there will be an escape ramp available.

Tire failure is another potential emergency. A banging or booming sound will usually alert the driver when a tire goes out. Truck wheels may also start to vibrate, causing the entire vehicle to shake. Another sign that a tire has blown out is if the steering wheel suddenly tightens up. When tire failure occurs, the driver should firmly grasp the steering wheel and hold on. They need to allow the CMV to slow down without immediately applying the brakes. Once the truck has nearly come to a stop, they should pull off the road and apply the brakes. Then they should exit the vehicle and inspect all tires to see which one blew out. Ideally, the CMV will have at least one spare tire, allowing them to change it out. If this isn't possible, they need to call the vehicle insurer and report the tire outage. Many insurers will send out an emergency technician to help.

Antilock Braking Systems (ABS)

An antilock braking system (ABS) keeps the wheels from locking after braking too hard. It is a system separate from the normal brakes, and it has no effect on them. This system helps to maintain control of the CMV. It also helps to prevent skidding. An ABS has sensors that can tell right when the brakes are about to lock. Within that system is an electronic control unit (ECU) that will lighten up the pressure on the brakes.

The following types of vehicles are required to have ABSs:

- Tractor trailers that were built with air brakes on or after March 1, 1997
- Air brake trucks that were manufactured on or after March 1, 1998
- 10,000 lb.+ vehicles with hydraulic brakes that were manufactured on or after March 1, 1999

To figure out whether the CMV has an ABS, the driver can look for a yellow malfunction lamp on the left side of the truck. When a truck is first turned on, this light comes on for a few seconds. In older vehicles, it tends to stay on until the truck has driven a few miles. If the light does not go on, the ABS may no longer be functional.

On tractor trailers, an ABS may be built on either the tractor or the trailer. The placement of the ABS does not make it any more or less effective; it will work in either location. However, there are two key differences. An ABS on the tractor provides better steering control, while an ABS on the trailer prevents the trailer from swinging widely.

Driving a CMV with an ABS doesn't require special techniques. In fact, the way that a driver brakes while driving doesn't need to change. They just need to keep an eye on the malfunction lamp attached to the left of the vehicle. If the light stays on, indicating that the ABS isn't working, they shouldn't worry. The normal brakes will still work.

There are several things that an ABS will not do. It won't:

- alter the function of a vehicle's normal brakes
- improve or increase driving speed
- prevent skidding of wheels that are spun too quickly
- decrease stopping distance
- alter stopping ability
- substitute for regular brakes

Ideally, the ABS will only need to be used in an emergency. Drivers should drive at a safe speed, not make any sudden turns or increases in acceleration, and keep an appropriate amount of space between other vehicles so that there won't be a need to use the ABS.

Skid Control and Recovery

Over-accelerating, braking too hard, and steering too suddenly can all cause a truck to skid. Skidding occurs when tires lose traction on the road. This often happens when roads are icy, full of standing water, or snowy. When rear-drive wheels lock up from skidding, the CMV can tilt sideways. If this happens, a driver should stop braking immediately. Holding tightly to the steering wheel, they should steer in the opposite direction of how the truck has tilted. Once all wheels have returned to the road safely, they should counter-steer to straighten out.

Cargo that is too light to apply weight to the front axle of the vehicle and loss of tire tread also cause skidding. If these types of skidding occur, the driver needs to allow the vehicle to slow without applying too much pressure to the brakes. Once the CMV has slowed, they can find a safe area off-road and pull into it.

Skidding can be avoided. If a driver knows they are going to drive in inclement weather, they need to check the truck's tire tread ahead of time. If the tires appear worn down or "bald," it's time to replace them. If they can't replace them at the time, they should proceed carefully. When driving, they should not over-accelerate, and they should not slam on the brakes. Drivers should always drive slowly when roads are wet or icy.

Driving around curves puts drivers at higher risk for skidding. They should drive around them slowly. Drivers must never accelerate over the speed limit when driving around curves.

Defensive driving courses usually teach drivers how to handle skidding and pulling off the road. If they have the time or are simply curious, CMV drivers can consider taking one of these classes.

Accident Procedures

There are several things that a driver should do if an accident occurs. The first thing a driver should do, if they are able to get out of the vehicle, is survey the area. To avoid causing an even worse accident, they need to protect the scene. They should pull to the side of the highway and turn on their emergency lights. At some point, they need to call for help. They can do so before or after they get out of the CMV. While they are waiting for help to arrive, they can place reflective triangles in front of and behind the accident to warn other drivers.

The driver should check to see if anyone else was injured in the accident. An accident victim should be moved only if there is a chance of a fire starting or other danger. If there is no danger of a fire, the injured person should not be moved because doing so could cause further injury. If there are open wounds that

the driver can attend to, they should retrieve the first aid kit from their vehicle to use as necessary. Once the proper authorities arrive, the driver does not need to do anything further unless asked to. If they are asked to provide a statement, they should provide as much detail as they can about either their role in the accident or what they witnessed.

Even if the accident does not result in injuries, the driver should call the authorities. There will need to be a record of the incident in case either of the drivers discover other damages to their vehicles after driving away. The driver should take pictures of the scene of the accident in case the vehicle insurer needs them. The insurance company should be notified that an accident has occurred. If necessary, an attorney can be called. Before leaving the scene, the two drivers should exchange insurance information with each other.

Fires

There are several things that can cause CMV fires, including spilled or incorrectly used fuel, smoking while fueling up, damaged electrical systems, cargo that is highly flammable, and tires that aren't inflated enough. To prevent fires, drivers need to start by inspecting their trucks. They need to look for things that could possibly cause a fire, such as tires that are going flat and loose wires or other connections under the hood. When driving, they should periodically stop to check the temperature of their engine and tires; if the engine is smoking or the tires feel too hot, these are signs that a fire could start. When fueling up, drivers need to be careful not to spill any of the gas on themselves or on the sides of the vehicle.

Every truck should have a fire extinguisher that the driver can easily access if needed. They should learn how to use the extinguisher prior to driving. If a truck does catch fire, the first thing the driver needs to do is pull off the road as quickly and as safely as possible. They need to park away from other vehicles or any surroundings that could catch fire. It is not recommended that they pull into a filling station, as there will likely be spilled gas or other flammable substances surrounding the area. After pulling over, drivers need to grab the fire extinguisher and exit the vehicle. They should then use the extinguisher to put out as much of the fire as they can and call for help.

Keeping the fire from spreading is incredibly important. If the engine is on fire, the truck's hood should never be opened. The first thing the driver should do is turn the engine off and exit the vehicle. If the cargo is on fire, the driver should not open the doors to the truck in an attempt to put the cargo fire out. Doing so could result in the driver being burned or the ignition of the surrounding area.

There are two different types of fire extinguishers. If possible, drivers should have one of each. An ABC fire extinguisher usually puts out fires on cloth, paper, wood, or other fabrics. Water can be used on these types of fires. BC fire extinguishers usually put out fuel, liquid, or electrical fires. Water should never be thrown on these types of fires because it could cause electrocution or make the flames grow larger. When using an extinguisher, the person should stand upwind, a few feet away from the fire. It should be aimed at the base of the fire and not the flames.

Water can usually be used to put out fires on tires. If the driver is unsure of what to do, they should call the fire department and wait for them to put out the fire. The driver's safety is most important here, so they should not try to fight a fire if they are panicking.

Alcohol, Drugs, and Driving

Under no circumstances should anyone drive while under the influence of alcohol or other illicit substances. Being caught driving while under the influence can result in fines, jail time, and immediate

suspension of the person's driver's license. CDL drivers will be immediately disqualified if they show up on test day while intoxicated.

Drinking and driving is a leading cause of accidents. In the United States alone, it has resulted in over twenty thousand deaths annually. Alcohol affects a person's reaction time, vision, coordination, and perception. Inhibitions are lowered and judgment is greatly skewed when a person drinks alcohol. People's tolerance levels for alcohol vary, but all it takes is one drink to alter the senses.

The amount of alcohol in the bloodstream is measured by the blood alcohol concentration (BAC). The higher the BAC, the more intoxicated a person becomes. After entering the blood, alcohol is sent to the brain. Some of the alcohol is excreted in breath, sweat, and urine, but the remainder goes directly to the liver. The liver can only dispose of a tiny amount of alcohol.

Two people can drink the same amount of alcohol and have different BACs. This happens because BAC is affected by weight and how fast someone drinks, not just by the amount they drink. The higher the BAC, the less control the person has over their actions and thought processes. Because of how long it takes for them to feel the effects of alcohol, many people don't realize they are impaired. This is dangerous because those same people are likely to believe that is it safe for them to drive.

Impaired drivers tend to take more risks on the road and fail to adhere to traffic rules. Some may drive faster than they should, while others believe that driving slowly will help them evade the authorities. One of the most common things impaired drivers do is weave between traffic lanes.

Alcohol isn't the only substance that can affect a person's driving ability. There are many types of drugs, including marijuana and barbiturates, that are dangerous when consumed by drivers. Not all drugs are illegal; even over the counter and prescribed medications can impair drivers when taken incorrectly or in excess. If a driver is prescribed a medication with a warning label, such as "can cause drowsiness," they should consult with their doctor about whether it is safe to drive while taking it. Medications should always be taken as prescribed. If a driver is feeling tired or agitated after taking their prescriptions, they should not get behind the wheel and should instead get some rest.

Most medications come with a list of side effects. However, some side effects that are not included in the prescription's description might be experienced. If necessary, a medical professional should be contacted if a person has questions about side effects they are having. The local pharmacist is a valuable resource when a doctor can't be reached; a person can simply call them up and discuss the side effects that they are experiencing.

There are many myths about people being able to sober up by drinking lots of water, eating food, and taking cold showers. None of these methods truly work. Time is the only thing that sobers people up. Under no circumstances should a driver get behind the wheel if they are impaired by drugs or alcohol. To be safe, they can always reschedule their CDL test for a later date if they have consumed any of these substances.

Hazardous Materials Rules for All Commercial Drivers

CMV drivers sometimes transport hazardous materials. These materials are risky for the health and safety of the driver and the vehicle. If not handled properly, potentially irreparable damage can occur to the driver or their property.

Some hazardous materials are deadly. It's important that they are contained and labeled effectively. Caution must be taken when loading and unloading these products. The following are some examples of hazardous products:

- Flares
- Gasoline
- Propane
- Dynamite
- Battery fluid
- Fireworks
- Phosphorous

The company that ships the products is responsible for labeling them. These labels are usually yellow, diamond-shaped stickers or brightly colored tags. These products often come with a bit of paperwork describing the risks they pose. This paperwork must be read through before handling the products in order to know the best way to transport them and to ensure the driver's own protection. The papers need to be kept handy in case the driver is stopped by authorities who question them about their cargo. Keeping them in the glove compartment, on the passenger seat in a folder, or in a pouch with a zipper is best.

Drivers may use placards when transporting hazardous products. These placards are placed on the outside of the vehicle and are clearly visible to passersby. Just like the warning labels, these placards are usually brightly colored and diamond shaped. They also have codes that represent different types of hazards. The Department of Transportation offers an emergency guidebook that lists hazardous materials and their corresponding codes. Drivers can check their state's CMV manual for guidance on the use of placards.

If a CMV driver begins to transport hazardous materials regularly, their license needs to show a hazardous materials endorsement (HME). There is a written exam for this designation. Also, if their CMV has a cargo tank, they need a tank endorsement. Anyone driving a vehicle with placards must have the HME. It is against the law to drive without one. If a driver is caught without it, they will receive a citation.

CMV drivers should not hesitate to ask questions about hazardous cargo. They need to know as much information as possible to ensure safe delivery of these products.

Practice Quiz

1. What does CDL stand for?
    a. Certified driver's license
    b. Commercial driving license
    c. Controlled driving license
    d. Commercial driver's license

2. How much pressure should a CMV's air gauge be able to build to?
    a. 120-140 psi
    b. 130-140 psi
    c. 120-160 psi
    d. 160-180 psi

3. How much tread depth should properly inflated steering tires have?
    a. 2/32 inches
    b. 4/30 inches
    c. 4/32 inches
    d. 3/34 inches

4. Which statement about steering is the most accurate?
    a. It is acceptable to steer with one hand.
    b. The wheel should always turn 360 degrees when backing up.
    c. Both hands should be on the steering wheel in the 10:00 and 2:00 positions.
    d. You should let go of the steering wheel and clutch if a collision occurs.

Answer Explanations

1. D: CDL stands for commercial driver's license.

2. A: The air gauge must be able to build to 120-140 psi.

3. C: Choice *C* is correct because properly inflated steering tires should have a tread depth of 4/32 inches. The remaining tires must have a tread depth of 2/32 inches.

4. C: Choice *C* is correct; you should always drive with your hands in the 10:00 and 2:00 positions on the steering wheel. Choice *A* is incorrect because you should not steer with one hand. Choice *B* is incorrect because turning the wheel 360 degrees would be incredibly dangerous. Choice *D* is incorrect because letting go of the wheel and clutch during a collision could make it worse.

Transporting Cargo and Passengers Safely

Inspecting Cargo

It's a good idea to inspect cargo as a road trip progresses, not just before getting on the road. Make sure the cargo is fastened securely or properly loaded onto the truck. If locks, chains, or belts are used to hold the cargo in place, they should be closed properly. If the cargo is stacked in the back of the vehicle, make sure it is secured so that it does not slide around or hit against the back doors of the truck.

Cargo should be checked after the first 50 miles and then again after 150 miles or when 3 hours have passed. After that, every time the vehicle is stopped somewhere, such as at a rest station, check the cargo. It is easy for cargo to move around or belts to become loose while driving. Weight limits and cargo security requirements vary; at a minimum, drivers should check the requirements for every state they will be driving through.

Weight and Balance

Overloading vehicles can be dangerous. It is important for drivers to know the weight limit of every CMV they drive. Usually, the truck's manufacturer will specify the gross vehicle weight rating (GVWR), so check the driver's manual for this information if it is not otherwise displayed. There are GVWRs for the power and towing units of every CMV; the sum of these weights is the gross combination weight rating (GCWR).

Vehicle manufacturers also post weight specifications for the following parts of a CMV:

- axles
- tires
- suspension systems
- coupling devices

In addition to the weight requirements provided by manufacturers, individual states have their own legal CMV weight allowances. Also, a bridge formula is used to determine maximum weights for axles. Axles that are closer together often require less weight.

An overloaded truck can cause numerous problems. When driving downhill, the vehicle could descend faster than the driver can manage. Too much weight affects ascension, causing the CMV to slow down when the driver is trying to accelerate. Too much weight can also cause the brakes to work harder than intended, which can result in brake failure. The ability to stop during inclement weather is also worsened when cargo is too heavy.

How cargo is stacked on a truck is extremely important when it comes to balance. Uneven stacks or those that are stacked too high or too much to one side can cause a CMV to tip over. Balance also affects steering. To ensure proper balance, make sure there is an even amount of cargo across the back of the CMV as well as on the sides and down the middle of the trailer.

Securing Cargo

There are a few different ways that drivers can secure their cargo. The following sections briefly explain each one.

Blocking and Bracing

Blocking and bracing involves using custom-fitted metal or wooden planks to hold cargo. These planks should be placed on all sides of the cargo to keep it from moving, and they should be bolted to the cargo deck.

Tie-Downs

Tie-downs are straps that can be adjusted to fit around cargo. For CMVs that do not have enclosed trailers, tie-downs keep products from falling off the truck. Using them inside enclosed trailers helps keep cargo from shifting. Tie-downs can also be made of chains or rope, and they must have hooks, rings, bolts, or other attachments that "lock" them in place. There are legal weight and length restrictions for tie-downs, so check local trucking rules.

Header Boards

Also known as "headache racks," header boards prevent cargo from moving in the event of an accident. These racks are usually placed directly behind the back window behind the driver.

Covers

It's a good idea to cover cargo to protect it from spills and weather damage. Covers can be secured with tie-downs. Keep an eye on the cargo while driving to make sure it's still wrapped tightly around the shipment and doesn't blow off.

Containers

Shipping containers are frequently used to transport cargo. They typically come in standard sizes that fit ships, trains, and CMVs. They are typically secured by locks, bolts, or tie-downs. Before loading a shipping container, make sure they meet specified axle weight limits.

Cargo That Requires Special Attention

Some types of cargo require special accommodations to be transported safely. These include dry bulk, hanging meat, livestock, and oversized loads.

Dry bulk cargo can include coffee, grains, raw minerals, metals, and produce. As the name implies, these items are transported in bulk and must be kept dry. During shipping, these products are kept in unpackaged parcels, so they must be loaded in a way that prevents them from shifting during transport. Drive carefully to keep these shipments from falling off the truck.

Transporting hanging meat isn't easy. A refrigerated truck must be used, and swift moves on the road, such as sharp turns, must be avoided. Drive slowly so that the meat does not fall off the hooks.

Use extra care when transporting livestock. Animals move around a lot, making it harder to transport them safely and causing the shipment to be unbalanced. If the number of animals being shipped is sparse, the driver should include false bulkheads that cause the animals to move closer together. To prevent the vehicle from flipping over, be careful not to overload the sides.

A special permit must be obtained to transport an oversized load. Shipment of these loads is often limited to specific hours. Drivers may be required to use flashing lights, "wide load" signs, or other markers to warn passersby not to drive too close to the CMV. At times, police and non-police escorts are used to help drivers safely get a shipment to its intended location.

Transporting Passengers Safely

Anyone driving a bus or other vehicle that seats sixteen or more people must obtain a CDL that displays a passenger endorsement. Passenger endorsements are provided after drivers pass applicable knowledge and skills tests, which vary from state to state.

Passenger safety is of the utmost importance. Drivers should ensure that passengers stay seated with their seat belts fastened whenever the vehicle is in motion. If they are in the trailer portion of a CMV for any reason, they should never stand up when the truck is in motion. Passengers should never open doors while the CMV is being driven, even at a stop sign. When exiting the vehicle, advise passengers to watch their step.

Irritating passenger behavior should also be kept to a minimum. A passenger who is being too loud, putting feet up on the dashboard, and constantly changing the radio station or temperature inside of the vehicle can distract the driver and cause an accident. Advise passengers to avoid adjusting mirrors without permission. They should also not wear any clothing that could reflect sunlight into the driver's eyes.

Rules drivers might have about eating, smoking, talking on cell phones, or other potentially distracting behavior should be communicated to passengers before taking off.

Vehicle Inspection

Before departing with passengers in tow, make sure the CMV is safe. Inspect all brakes, tires, lights, windshield wipers, and mirrors. Make sure the steering wheel isn't wobbly or making unusual noises when turned. Test the horn. Ensure that all emergency equipment, including reflectors and fire extinguishers, is in place.

Emergency exits and access panels should be closed prior to taking off. If driving a bus, make sure the aisles are clean and clear of obstacles. Stairs to get on and off the vehicle should be clean as well. If there are hand railings and emergency exit handles, they should be secured so that they are not easily removed. There must be visible emergency exit signs. Passenger seats should be tightly secured so that they don't move when the vehicle is in motion. Of course, seat belts should also be functional and intact. If the vehicle has an emergency roof hatch, make sure it is closed.

Loading and Trip Start

If passengers have carry-on luggage, it should not be left in the aisles, in front of doors, or anywhere that the driver or other passengers could trip over it. All baggage should be secured in a separate area in luggage holders or at the back of the vehicle. Baggage should not be in areas where it could potentially fall on passengers or the driver and cause injury.

In the event of an emergency, passengers should be able to access all exit points, including windows. Do not transport hazardous materials inside the vehicle where people are seated. Hazardous materials, including corrosives, explosives, gasses, and flammable substances such as fuel and poisons, must be transported in the trailer portion of a CMV; they cannot be transported on a bus. For a complete table of hazardous materials, visit the Code of Federal Regulations website at www.ecfr.gov.

Bus drivers are not permitted to transport certain hazardous materials. Liquid Class 6 poisons and tear gas, for example, cannot be transported by bus. Radioactive products, small arms, and explosives can't be transported in spaces containing passengers. If passengers board a bus carrying hazardous materials, the materials must be labeled as such. They can't bring gasoline or car batteries on board a bus.

Some buses allow passengers to stand up, and they have lines in the aisle to show how far back a passenger must stand from the driver's seat. These lines are called *standee lines*. A standing passenger is prohibited from standing in front of this line.

It is important for bus drivers to announce their stops for passenger awareness. They should announce the location, the reason for stopping, when they will depart, and the bus number. Remind any departing passengers to take their belongings with them and watch their step as they exit. If driving a charter bus, do not allow anyone on the bus before it's time to depart; this can prevent vandalism of the bus or theft of passenger belongings.

On the Road

When driving a bus, always announce the road rules. These can range from not allowing eating or smoking to rules about the noise level.

Not only should bus drivers keep an eye on the road and surroundings, but they should also keep an eye on the inside of the bus. It is important for drivers to make sure that passengers keep their extremities inside the bus while it's moving and speak up if someone violates the rules.

When preparing to stop, instruct passengers to stay seated until the vehicle has fully stopped. If they're getting off the vehicle, advise them to watch their step so they don't trip. Before departing again, advise passengers to sit down.

When dealing with a disruptive passenger, it is important to maintain composure. Arguing with a passenger is pointless and could escalate the situation. Drivers should wait until they are in a safe location to ask a passenger to get off the bus. Make sure the drop-off location is well lit and that other people are present. Do not touch the disruptive person. If driving a bus with multiple exits, open all of them so that the person has more than one option to get off the bus. For passengers who refuse to exit, drivers should call their immediate supervisor or, if necessary, the authorities.

If a bus is involved in an accident, the driver should stay calm and call for help. The most common bus accidents involve incorrectly crossing intersections, scraping other vehicles when driving past them, and underestimating the amount of clearance a bus needs to go under different structures, such as bridges. Keep the amount of space the bus needs for clearance and accelerating between other vehicles in mind. It's impossible to know how other drivers will react on the road; each driver can only control their own driving and stay alert.

Driving around curves, especially in rain, sleet, or snow, is very dangerous. Do not speed around curves as this could cause the bus to roll over or skid off the road. Proceed cautiously, never overaccelerating. Going a few miles below the posted speed limit is usually the best practice for bus drivers.

Never cross a railroad crossing without looking in both directions and listening for oncoming trains. Stop 15 to 50 feet before the crossing and open the forward door of the bus in order to see and hear better. If railroad signals are lit up, do not cross. Look out for police, signs, or other signals. When it is safe to cross the tracks, do not shift gears when directly over them. Drive slowly and steadily until the entire bus has crossed the railroad.

Always come to a complete stop, approximately 50 feet away, when approaching a drawbridge. If there is a signal or an attendant, wait until the drawbridge has completely closed and the signal or attendant says it's safe to cross.

After-Trip Vehicle Inspection

Always inspect the vehicle after each trip. Some carriers require drivers to submit a full report at the end of each day. List the name and/or number of the bus, any issues that were encountered, and any other highlights of driving the vehicle that day. Drivers must report all damage to the vehicle, whether it was their fault or that of the passengers. Make sure all interlocks and signaling devices still work.

Review everything that was inspected prior to departure. If there are no issues to report, note it.

Prohibited Practices

The following are behaviors that drivers should avoid when operating a bus or other passenger vehicle.

- While riders are on board, do not fuel up the vehicle.
- Do not engage in lengthy discussions with passengers or any other distracting activities.
- Unless it's not safe for passengers to get off, do not have the vehicle towed or moved while they are on board if the vehicle is disabled. Drivers' employers should have instructions for what to do if their vehicle breaks down.

Use of Brake-Door Interlocks

Brake-door interlocks, also known as accelerator interlocks, are activated when a vehicle's rear door opens while its throttle is idle. The interlocks deactivate when the rear door closes. Mass transit buses usually have these systems. Please note that interlocks do not take the place of parking brakes.

Practice Quiz

1. What does a driver who is going to transport passengers need to acquire?
    a. Passenger endorsement
    b. An HME
    c. Medical documentation
    d. Reflectors

2. Which three parts make up the air brakes?
    a. Head, block, and oil sump
    b. Axle beam, swivel pin, and track load
    c. Emergency, service, and parking brakes
    d. Ball joints, stub axle, and drag link

3. Which of the following is a hazardous material?
    a. Antifreeze
    b. Ash
    c. Grinding dust
    d. Pesticide

4. Which of the following medical conditions would NOT need to be documented for a driver who has a CDL?
    a. Diabetes
    b. Hypertension
    c. Sinusitis
    d. Vertigo

5. What is an out-of-service order?
    a. An order to temporarily stop operating a CMV
    b. An order to turn in a CDL
    c. A notification that a CMV needs repair
    d. A notification that a CMV driver is out sick

Answer Explanations

1. A: A driver who plans to transport passengers must acquire a passenger endorsement. Choice *B* is incorrect because an HME is a hazardous materials endorsement, which is needed to transport hazardous products. Choice *C* is incorrect because medical documentation is not required to transport passengers. Choice *D* is incorrect because reflectors have nothing to do with transporting passengers; they help make vehicles more visible on the highway.

2. C: The air brakes include the emergency, service, and parking brakes. Choice *A* is incorrect; the head, the block, and the oil sump are parts of an engine. Choice *B* is incorrect because an axle beam, swivel pin, and track load are part of a front axle. Choice *D* is incorrect; ball joints, stub axle, and drag link are part of the steering system.

3. D: Pesticide is a hazardous material. Antifreeze, ash, and grinding dust are not hazardous materials.

4. C: Sinusitis does not need to be documented for a driver with a CDL. The remaining choices are incorrect because diabetes, hypertension, and vertigo all require medical documentation for CDL drivers.

5. A: An out-of-service order is an order to stop operating a CMV temporarily.

Air Brakes

Parts of an Air Brake System

Air brakes work using compressed air. They consist of three braking systems: emergency, service, and parking. Many CMVs use the air brake system, which has the following components.

Air Compressor and Air Compressor Governor

Air compressors push air into storage tanks. Gears connect the compressor to the engine, and it is lubricated by engine oil. The engine cooling system also cools the air compressor.

The amount of air pumped into the storage tank is controlled by the compressor governor. The maximum amount of air pressure that can be pumped into a storage tank is 125 psi. If the air compression drops to 100 psi, the compressor can begin pumping air into the storage tank again.

Storage Tanks

Compressed air is held in storage tanks. Different CMVs have tanks of various sizes. Air brakes can work multiple times using the air within the tanks.

Tank Drains

Water and oil can collect in air compressors, which isn't good for air brakes. Water, in particular, can freeze inside the tanks and cause them to break. For this reason, storage tanks come with drain valves to allow these substances to exit the tanks. These valves are usually manual or automatic. Manual valves must be opened and emptied every day. Automatic drains get rid of oil and water on their own. Some automatic tank drains come with electric heating devices that also keep tanks from freezing.

Alcohol Evaporator

An alcohol evaporator pumps alcohol into air brake systems, preventing ice from building up in them. In the winter months, it may be necessary to fill the alcohol container every day. The storage tank will also need to be drained daily.

Safety Valve

Inside the air brake storage tank is a safety valve. This valve restricts the amount of pressure that can be pumped into the tank, preventing it from being overfilled. If the pressure reaches 150 psi, the safety valve will open and require repair.

Brake Pedal

The brake pedal is also known as the foot valve. The amount of air pressure applied to the brakes depends on how hard the driver pushes on it. More pushing equals more pressure, and less pushing equals less pressure. Less pressure releases the brakes and reduces the amount of air collected in the air brake tanks. There must be just enough pressure for the brakes to work; if there isn't, the brakes will fail.

Foundation Brakes

There is a foundation brake at the end of each wheel axle. They are made up of the following parts:

- **Drums, shoes, and linings:** These parts work together. The shoes and linings are inside the drum and are pushed together when braking to help a vehicle stop.
- **S-cam brakes:** These brakes are activated when air enters the brake chamber, forcing the camshaft to twist. Brake shoes move apart and push against the inside of the brake drum.
- **Wedge brakes:** These brakes, which have a single- or double-brake chamber, wedge between two brake shoes and push them away from each other.
- **Disc brakes:** With these brakes, a power screw fastens a disc between brake pads.

Supply Pressure Gauges

Pressure gauges are attached to all air tanks. Gauges measure the amount of air pressure in tanks.

Application Pressure Gauge

Application pressure gauges tell the driver how much air pressure is being put on the brakes. Too much pressure is a sign that brakes are about to fail or need repair.

Low Air–Pressure Warning

This warning alerts the driver when air pressure in the brakes has dropped below 60 psi. It may be accompanied by a buzzer, a mechanical arm called a *wig wag,* or a red light. For charter buses, the alert may come on when pressure has been reduced to 80-85 psi.

Stop-Light Switch

When the brakes are applied, an electric switch powered by air pressure turns on this light. It alerts other drivers that the vehicle is slowing down or stopping.

Front Brake Limiting Valve

These valves are installed in most vehicles to prevent the front wheels from skidding while reducing the brakes' power to stop. They reduce the amount of air that can reach the front brakes. These valves have been shown to work on some of the most slippery road conditions, including those with ice, rain, and sleet. Please note that the driver does not control front brake limiting valves.

Spring Brakes

When air pressure is suddenly removed from air brakes by a leak or other issue, spring brakes activate, acting as emergency brakes. Heavy-duty vehicles, such as buses, truck tractors, and most trucks, have spring brakes. If air pressure drops to between 20 and 45 psi, these brakes will activate.

Parking Brake Controls

Parking brakes are separate from the rest of a vehicle's brakes, and they only control the rear brakes. They are usually controlled by a knob that the driver first pulls and then releases to activate them. It is imperative not to apply pressure to the brake pedal when using the parking brake.

Parking brakes either have modulating control valves or dual parking control valves. Modulating valves have controls located on dashboards. The force of the brake depends on the amount of pressure applied (in other words, how hard it is pulled) to the modulating valve.

Dual parking control valves use pressure from a separate air tank to activate the spring brakes. They are used in emergency situations when it is necessary to park or move. The air supply can run out, so these valves should be used sparingly.

Anti-Lock Braking System

An anti-lock braking system (ABS) is required for the following vehicles:

- Air brake–equipped truck tractors built after March 1, 1997
- Other air brake–equipped vehicles built after March 1, 1998

If there is an issue with the ABS, a yellow malfunction lamp or warning light will light up. These lights are located either in the front or rear corners of vehicles or on their instrument panels. The light will go out immediately on newer vehicles but will stay on in older ones operating at a speed of less than 5 mph. If the light does not go out, repair may be required because the ABS for the wheels may be broken.

Under no circumstances does the ABS take the place of a vehicle's normal brakes. The ABS comes on when it detects that the wheels are going to lock up. It helps the driver maintain control of the vehicle.

Dual Air Brake

Dual air brakes are installed on heavy vehicles, such as trucks, tractor trailers, and buses. There are two air brake systems, complete with their own tanks and other parts. They independently operate the front and rear axles. Although they are separate systems, they use the same brake controls.

Both air systems need to have 100 psi of pressure before the vehicle can be driven. A gauge warning light and/or buzzer will activate if there isn't enough air pressure. The driver should pull over if these warning signs are activated. This is an indication that the front or rear brakes are out of service. The light and/or buzzer will turn off when the pressure has reached at least 60 psi.

Inspecting Air Brake Systems

There are seven steps in the air brake inspection process:

1. Test the low-air warning device.
2. Check the air pressure buildup.
3. Test the governor cut-out.
4. Test the governor cut-in.
5. Check the air-loss rate.
6. Check the service brakes.
7. Test the spring brakes.

The CDL test will focus on just a few of these steps. Continue reading to figure out which steps you should study the most.

Step 2: Check the air pressure buildup. When doing this, it is necessary to determine if the air compressor is belt-driven. If it is, make sure that the belt is tight and in good condition.

Step 5: Check the air-loss rate. While parked on level ground, place a sturdy material, such as rubber, in front of the vehicle's wheels to keep it from rolling. Do a walk-around inspection. Then, release the parking brakes. Apply pressure to the service brakes to listen for any air that may be leaking out. No more than 4 psi should be lost per minute. This is also the time to make sure that air hoses do not have any cuts

or holes in them and that they are connected properly. In addition, there should not be any damage to brake drums or linings.

Step 7: Test the spring brakes. These brakes are tested by driving forward for approximately 1 yard and then applying the spring/parking brake. Notice if there are any issues activating the brake. Check the air pressure gauge to make sure the pressure is at least 100 psi.

Test the air leakage rate by turning off the vehicle and then pulling the spring/parking brake. Single vehicles should lose air no more than 2 psi per minute, and combination vehicles should lose no more than 3 psi per minute.

Next, trigger the low-pressure warning signal to see if it works. This is done by stepping on and off the brake while the electrical power is on and the engine is off. The goal is to trigger the warning signal to appear when the pressure is nearing 60 psi.

It is also important to see if air pressure builds quickly enough within the spring brakes. Single vehicles should see a buildup of 85 to 100 psi within 45 seconds. Combination vehicles should see 50 to 90 psi within 3 minutes. Air pressure that does not build quickly is a sign that the brakes need repair. Pull over and call a tow service.

Using Air Brakes

Finally, but most importantly, the following covers how to properly use air brakes.

Making Normal Stops

To come to a normal stop, simply push down on the brake pedal. Do not slam on the brakes. Apply just enough pressure to come to a slow, safe stop. For manual transmissions, wait until the engine idles before pulling the clutch.

Using Anti-Lock Brakes

The ABS shouldn't be triggered unless the wheels lock up. The system is automatic, so there is no need to try to trigger them. Brake normally. It is good to have the ABS checked to ensure that it will activate if necessary. If the ABS fails, keep pushing the regular brakes and try to come to a safe stop.

Emergency Stops

What if a driver cuts off another driver in traffic or stops in front of a driver abruptly? To avoid an accident, drivers should either use controlled braking or the stab-braking method.

Controlled braking is when the brakes are pushed forcefully, but the wheels do not lock up. Instead of jerking the steering wheel too far in one direction, steer with small motions in a controlled manner. Try to keep the vehicle as straight as possible.

The stab-braking method is employed when the brakes are pushed all the way down to the car floor. This is a hard, sudden movement, but steering should remain smooth and controlled. Let go of the steering wheel if the tires lock up, and then promptly press down the brakes again.

Air Brakes

Stopping Distance

The amount of time it takes the brakes to activate after being pushed is called *brake lag*. Consider brake lag when estimating stopping distance. Air brakes sometimes take a few seconds to activate. When incorporating brake lag, the calculation for stopping distance is as follows:

Reaction distance + perception distance + braking distance + brake lag = stopping distance

Practice Quiz

1. Which of the following is NOT part of the air brake system?
    a. Air compressor governor
    b. Safety valve
    c. Tank drains
    d. Pistons

2. What is the maximum amount of air pressure allowed in a storage tank?
    a. 150 psi
    b. 125 psi
    c. 100 psi
    d. 85 psi

3. What does it mean to "chock" wheels?
    a. Add compressed air to them.
    b. Put material in front of them to keep them from moving.
    c. Rotate them every 3,000 miles.
    d. Replace the wheels after every long-haul road trip.

4. Which of the following is used as a low air pressure alert symbol?
    a. A yellow light
    b. A bell
    c. A wig wag
    d. A whistle

Answer Explanations

1. D: Pistons are part of an engine. The remaining choices are incorrect because they are all part of the air brake system.

2. B: 125 psi is the maximum amount of air pressure allowed in a storage tank. Choice *A* is incorrect because 150 psi is over the maximum. Choice *C* is incorrect; if the air pressure drops to 100 psi, more air can be allowed into the storage tank. Choice *D* is incorrect because 85 psi would trigger a low-pressure warning.

3. B: Chocking is when material such as rubber is put in front of the wheels to keep them from moving.

4. C: A wig wag is a mechanical arm that displays air pressure levels. The remaining choices are incorrect because they are not low air pressure symbols.

Combination Vehicles

Driving Combination Vehicles Safely

Often larger than single vehicles, combination vehicles (single, double, and triple tractor-trailers, as well as straight trucks with fixed trailers) require specific knowledge and skill to operate. Their extra weight and length, as well as additional operational features, require special consideration when driving.

Rollover Risks

Compared to those with empty trailers, rigs with full loads are ten times more likely to roll over in a collision. As cargo weight is added in the trailer, the truck's center of gravity changes. This shift makes rollovers (a leading cause of driver death) more likely.

The two most important ways to reduce the risk of rollover are: 1) to position cargo low to the ground and centered left-to-right, and 2) to slow down when turning or otherwise changing direction.

Cargo placement is especially important in combination vehicles (see the image below). Cargo piled unnecessarily high or positioned to one side makes the trailer more likely to lean and roll. Placing extra cargo weight too close to the rear of the trailer increases the risk for trailer sway. Outside of collisions, changing directions too quickly can cause rollovers, especially with a full load. Drive cautiously and slowly, particularly when turning, taking on-ramps or off-ramps, and changing lanes.

Steering Gently

In a combination vehicle with a trailer, turning the steering wheel abruptly can lead to the "crack-the-whip" effect, which can cause the trailer to turn over. This effect is caused by "rearward amplification," whereby combination vehicles with longer trailers are more likely to roll over.

Combination Vehicles

The figure below shows how different sizes and combinations of trailers affect the risk of experiencing the crack-the-whip effect caused by rearward amplification. Combination vehicle types are shown from the least likely to roll at the top to the most likely to roll at the bottom of the chart. The rearward amplification value number at the top right shows the increased likelihood that the rearmost trailer of that setup will roll over compared to the likelihood that the tractor will roll over. For example, the conventional double setup with a rearward amplification of 2.0 means the rearmost trailer is two times more likely to turn over than the tractor.

To reduce the risk of this effect, steer combination vehicles with trailers gently and smoothly, especially when changing lanes or driving around curves. In addition to steering cautiously, always allow a safe following distance and look ahead on the road to prevent the need for fast braking. In a combination vehicle traveling below 40 mph, leave one second of following distance per 10 feet of vehicle length; when traveling over 40 mph, add an additional second. Look ahead when driving, not right in front of your vehicle. Exercise additional caution and drive more slowly when driving at night or making turns.

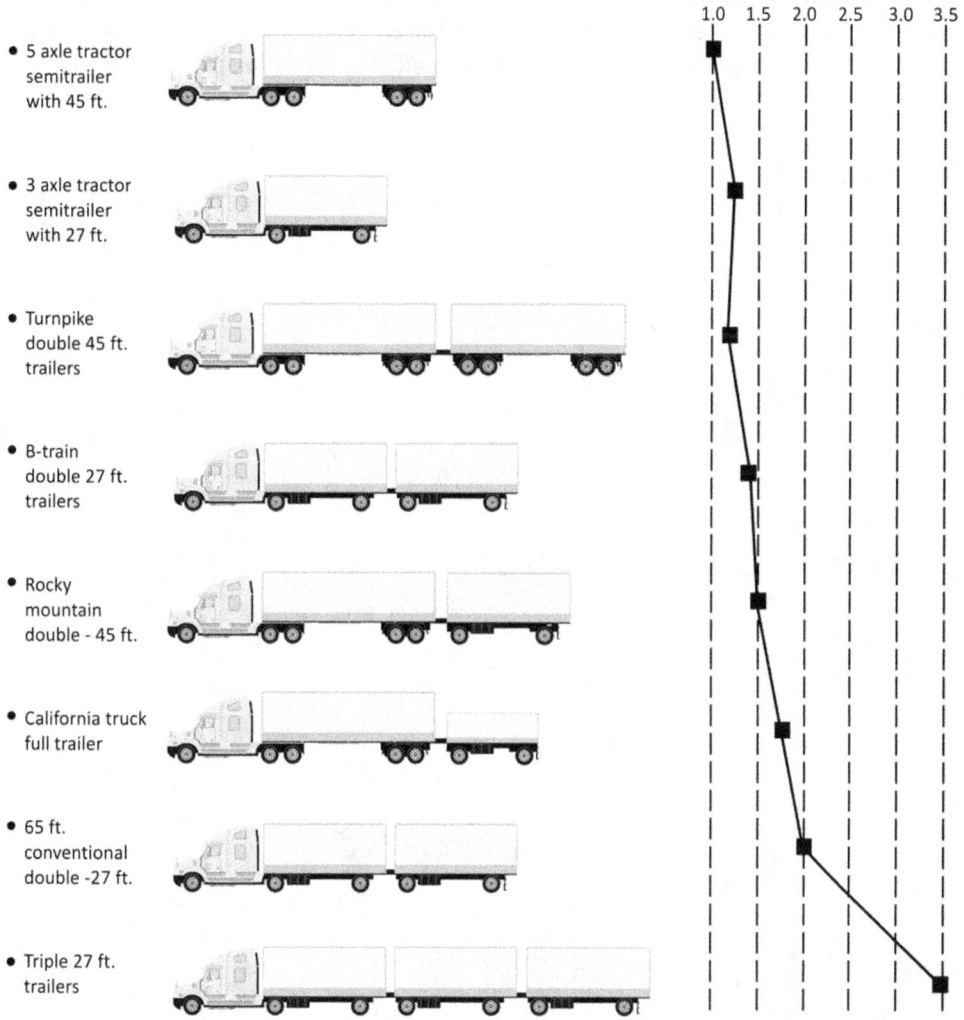

INFLUENCE OF COMBINATION TYPE ON REARWARD AMPLIFICATION

- 5 axle tractor semitrailer with 45 ft.
- 3 axle tractor semitrailer with 27 ft.
- Turnpike double 45 ft. trailers
- B-train double 27 ft. trailers
- Rocky mountain double - 45 ft.
- California truck full trailer
- 65 ft. conventional double -27 ft.
- Triple 27 ft. trailers

47

Combination Vehicles

Braking Early

In combination vehicles, slow, gentle braking is key to avoiding tractor swinging or a jackknife, whether or not the trailer is loaded. Unloaded or lightly loaded combination vehicles take longer to stop than those with loaded trailers. Their brakes and tight suspension springs make them especially prone to poor traction, wheels locking up, and significant trailer swinging or even a jackknife. Similarly, "bobtail" tractors with no trailers attached have been shown to take more time and effort to stop smoothly than heavily loaded tractor-trailer combination vehicles. Make slow, safe braking easier by minimizing the need for sudden stops. Allow distance between your vehicle and the one ahead of you, be attentive to surrounding activity, and keep your gaze ahead of you.

Railroad-Highway Crossings

Trailers, especially those with low underneath clearance, can get caught on railroad-highway crossings. Low trailers include lowboys, car carriers, moving vans, and possum-belly livestock trailers. A trailer with landing gear mistakenly set for a tandem-axle tractor is also at risk of getting stuck when being pulled by a single-axle tractor.

For your safety, immediately exit your vehicle if it becomes stuck on train tracks. Step away from the tracks before calling 911 or an emergency number. Look for emergency notification information on the railroad signal or nearby signage. When providing your location, give as much detail as possible and include the DOT number if available.

Preventing Trailer Skids

As mentioned above, empty or lightly loaded trailers are especially prone to their wheels locking up (skidding), which can cause the trailer to swing or even jackknife, as shown in the image below.

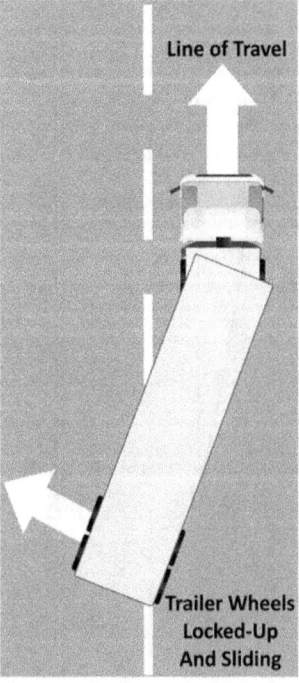
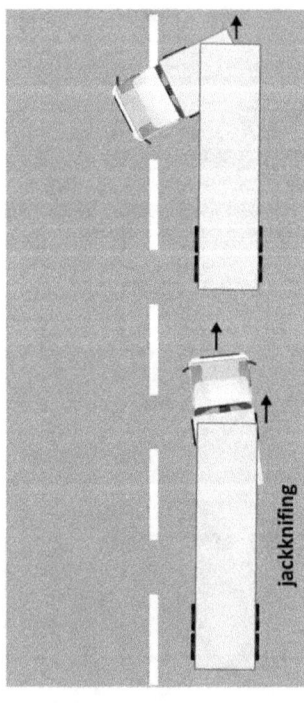
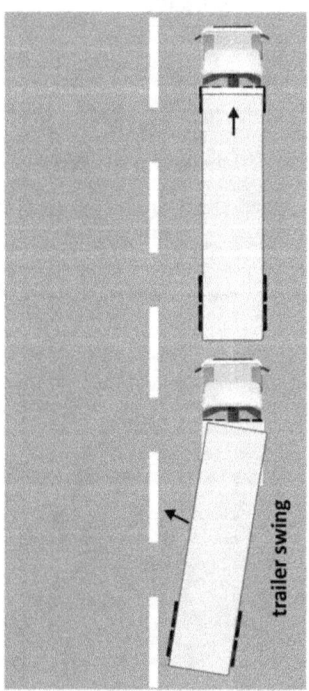

Combination Vehicles

When braking hard, it is a good practice to check your mirrors to ensure that the trailer is not swinging. When you see that motion, you are watching the trailer skid. Recognizing the skid is the first step in stopping it from getting out of control and possibly causing a jackknife. A trailer that has entered the lane next to you is very likely to jackknife.

Once you observe the skid, release the brakes. This allows the trailer wheels to regain traction, so the tractor can realign behind the trailer. Focus on steering as the trailer starts following behind the tractor. Avoid using the trailer hand valve, which will send air to the trailer brakes and may cause additional skidding.

Turning Wide

Off-tracking, or "cheating," is the name for a process in which the rear wheels of a rig follow behind the front wheels in a different path. Overall, the tractor in a combination vehicle will make a wider turn than the trailer (Figure 6.4), which can cause the trailer to collide with the curb or other objects. Off-tracking is more pronounced in the rear wheels of a trailer than in the motorized rear wheels of the tractor. The amount of off-tracking increases with the length of the vehicle, and the rear wheels of the last trailer in a multi-trailer rig will off-track the most.

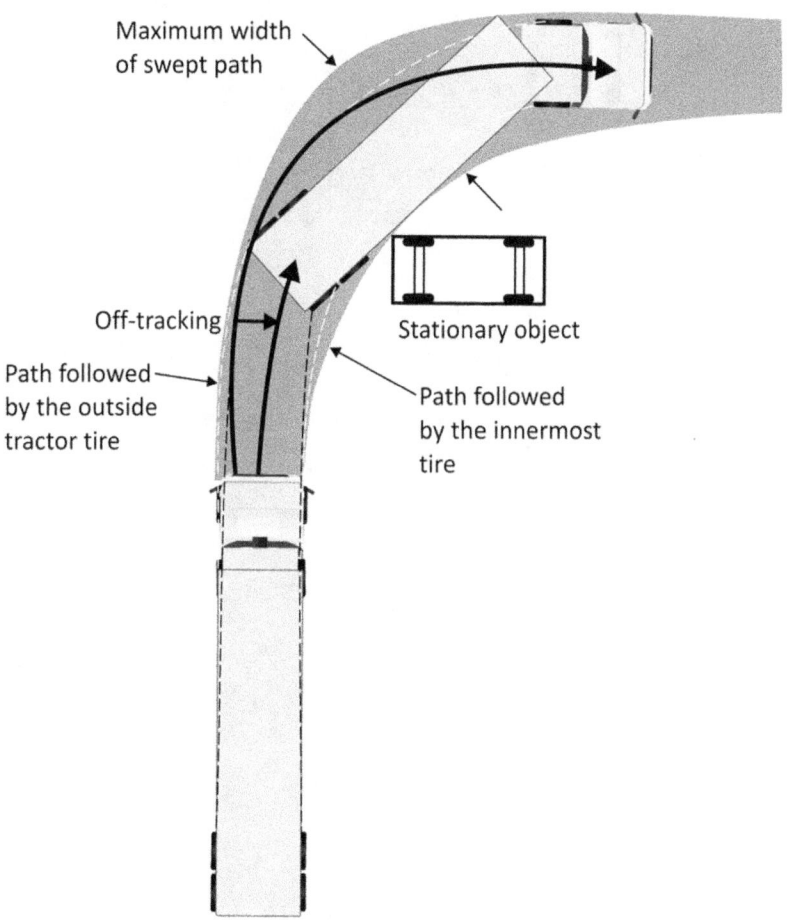

OFF-TRACKING IN A 90 DEGREE TURN

Combination Vehicles

Make wide turns around corners to compensate for off-tracking. Aim to keep the vehicle close to the curb to keep cars from passing on the right while also keeping the rear wheels from driving on the curb or possibly injuring pedestrians. If the turn requires you to enter another lane, use a button hook turn and swing wide during the turn, as displayed in the image below. Avoid jug handle turns, which swing wide before the turn; this may make other drivers think you are turning left and try to pass you.

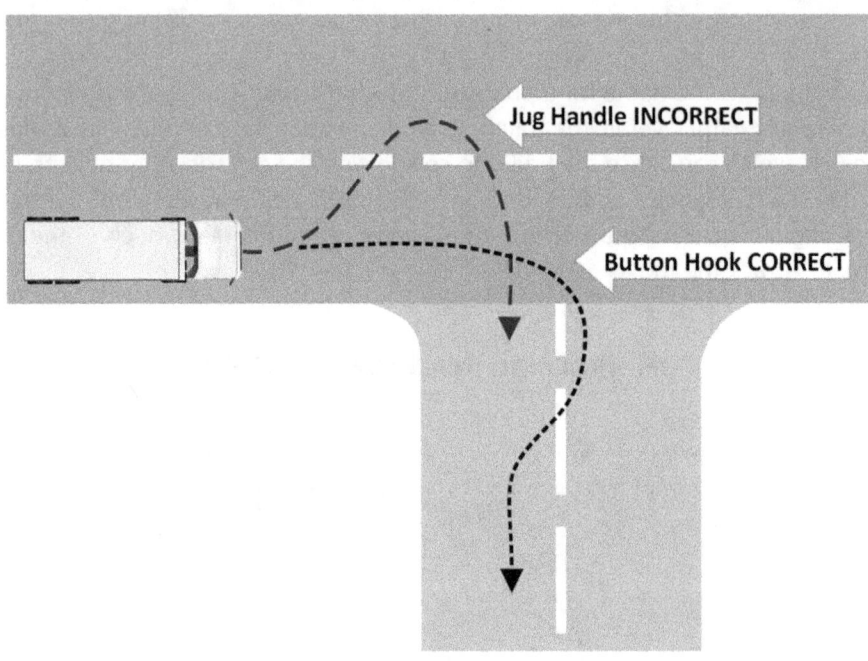

Backing with a Trailer

The easiest way to back a trailer is in a straight line. If backing in a curve is required, backing the trailer toward the driver side will make it easier to see. Unlike backing up in a car, straight truck, or bus, when backing a trailer, you first turn the steering wheel in the direction opposite from the direction you want to go. In other words, turning the steering wheel to the left sends the trailer to the right, and turning the steering wheel to the right sends the trailer to the left (see image below). After the trailer has started turning on your intended path, turn the steering wheel in the opposite direction, so the tractor follows the trailer.

If necessary, pull your rig forward at any time to correct your path.

To best prepare for backing a trailer, first exit your vehicle and walk around to locate any obstacles in your path. This will also allow you to see how much space you have over and around your vehicle.

While backing up, use your mirrors to check both sides of the vehicle as you move. Exit the vehicle to more closely assess your path and any obstacles as needed.

If your trailer begins to drift away from your intended path, turn the steering wheel toward the drift to correct it.

Combination Vehicle Air Brakes

This section expands on information in the earlier section on air brakes to include additional parts found in combination vehicles, where trailers have their own air brake systems.

Combination Vehicles

All trucks that pull trailers with air brakes have a tractor protection system made up of two valves: the tractor protection valve and the trailer air supply control valve. They protect the tractor's air supply if there is a loss of air in the trailer's braking system or the trailer becomes detached from the tractor.

Trailer Hand Valve
Whereas the foot brake pedal sends air to all brakes, including the tractor and trailer(s), the trailer hand valve (also called the trolley valve or Johnson bar) exclusively controls the trailer service brakes without engaging the brakes of the tractor.

The main purpose of the trailer hand valve is to test the brakes; it should not be used as a parking brake or to brake while driving. Using the trailer hand valve while driving can cause skidding by locking up the trailer wheels. If used for parking, the system may not be able to maintain air pressure for long periods of time. If the air leaks out and air pressure is lost, the brakes will fail if no spring brakes are present. Instead, use the parking brake and chock wheels on trailers that do not have spring brakes.

Tractor Protection Valve
The tractor protection valve maintains air in the tractor or truck brake system, even if there is an air leak or if the trailer becomes separated from the tractor. The "trailer air supply" control knob near the steering wheel manually controls the tractor protection valve. However, if pressure in the system falls to between 20 and 45 psi due to an air leak, the tractor protection valve will close automatically to stop air loss from the tractor. The valve closure also releases air from the trailer emergency line to engage the trailer's emergency brakes. If the emergency brakes engage while driving, the locked trailer wheels could cause trailer skidding.

Trailer Air Supply Control
To manually control the tractor protection valve, use the red, octagonal knob labeled "trailer air" on the dash. The trailer air supply controls the flow of air to the trailer by opening and closing the tractor protection valve. Pull the knob out to shut off air to the trailer and engage the trailer emergency brakes. Push the knob in to send air to the trailer, release the emergency brakes, and activate the service brakes.

When air pressure in the system falls to between 20 and 45 psi, the air supply control valve will automatically pop out to close the tractor protection valve. The trailer's spring brakes will come on automatically, and the yellow parking brake knob on the dash will also pop out. In older vehicles, the trailer air supply may be a lever with two positions: "normal," for sending air to the trailer during normal operation, and "emergency," to stop airflow to the trailer and engage its emergency brakes.

Trailer Air Lines

Trailer air lines connect the braking systems of the different parts of a combination vehicle (tractor, trailer[s], dollies, etc.). There are two air lines in combination vehicles: the service line, and the emergency line.

The **service air line** (also called the control or signal line) controls the service brakes, the brakes that stop the vehicle while driving. The driver controls air flow in the service line using the foot brake or the trailer hand brake. The air pressure in the service line changes with the amount of pressure that is applied to those brakes.

The service line carries the pressure from the service brake to relay valves in the trailer, which release air from the trailer air reservoir. The signal can travel the distance much faster than air from the tractor tanks, and braking response time is improved.

The **emergency air line** (or supply line) fills the trailer or dolly air tanks with air. It also releases the trailer's parking (emergency) brake. If the red line is damaged or becomes detached, and the air pressure drops, the tractor protection valve senses the air loss and turns on the emergency brake. The loss in pressure will also cause the air supply knob to pop out when the tractor protection valve closes. Air losses could result from the emergency air hose detaching or from a failure of any related parts.

The emergency hose, couplers, and related parts are usually colored red, while the service line is often colored blue. The image below shows how trailer service and emergency air lines operate trailer brakes.

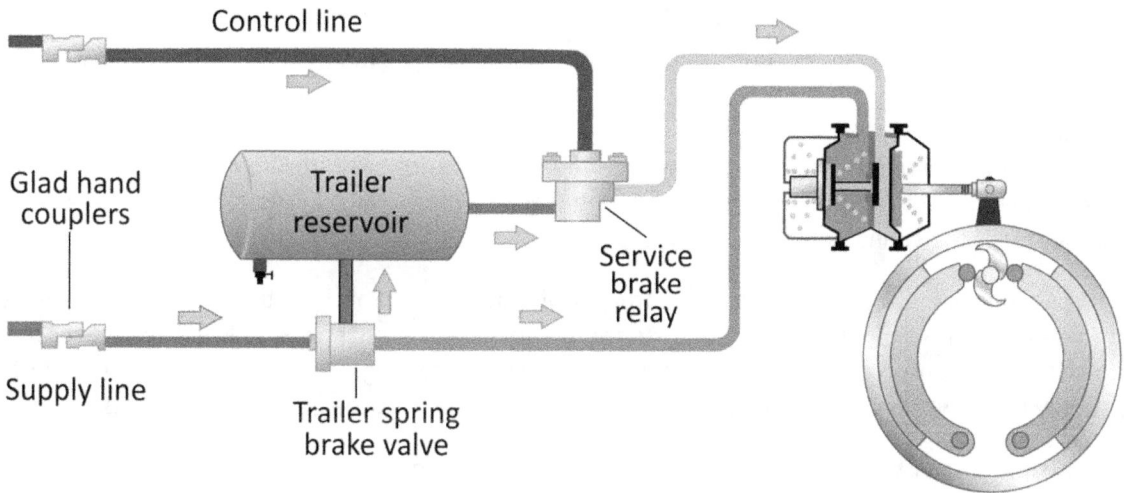

Hose Couplers (Glad Hands)

Hose couplers (glad hands) connect the service and emergency air lines from the tractor protection valve on the back of a tractor to the trailer. The couplers' rubber seals prevent air loss, so damaged or defective seals are a common cause of air loss in trailers.

Before connecting, inspect and clean the couplers and replace seals, as necessary. Connect the two rubber seals of the glad hands at a 90-degree angle and turn the hose coupler to lock in place. Truck air lines

Combination Vehicles

must be coupled with the correct trailer lines. Service lines are often colored blue or may have a metal "service" tag on them; emergency lines are often red or are labeled "emergency."

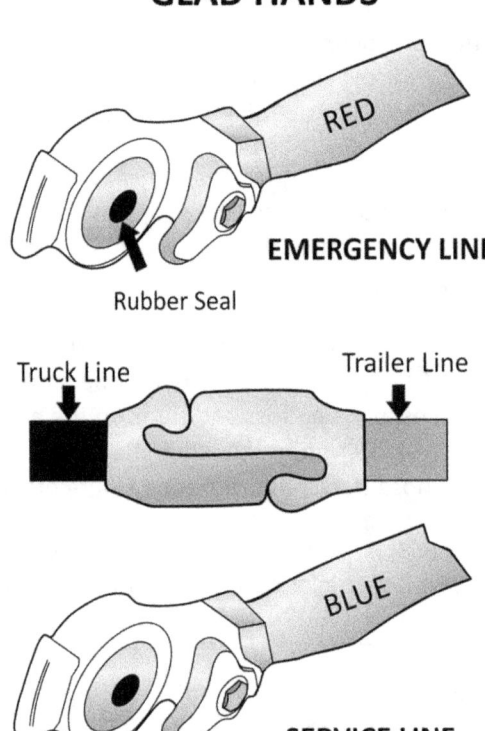

If the emergency air line is incorrectly connected to the service line on a trailer with spring brakes, the spring brakes will not release when you push the trailer air supply control. This is because there is no air in the tanks to lift the spring brakes.

Reversed air lines may not be so obvious in trailers without spring brakes, as the wheels will move freely. But there will be no air in the tanks to engage the service brakes on the trailer. Always test trailer brakes before driving to ensure that air tanks are full and brakes are working. Use the trailer hand valve or trailer air supply knob (which activates the tractor protection valve) in a low gear to test the brakes.

When air lines are not in use, glad hands should be connected to "dead end" or dummy couplers to keep the couplers and air lines clean. If no dummy couplers are available, glad hands may be used, which are designed to be linked together. They should always be stored in a way that keeps air lines clean and fully functional.

Trailer Air Tanks

Trailer and dolly air tanks store air that is used to provide air pressure needed to operate service brakes and keep the spring brakes off while driving. The emergency (supply) line from the tractor carries air to the air tanks, where it is stored until the service brakes—whether foot pedal or hand brake—are needed.

When the driver uses a service brake, the pressure applied is sent down the service line to the relay valves. Relay valves send air from the trailer air tanks to its brakes. The pressure applied to the brake pedal (or hand brake) indicates to the service line how much pressure should be sent to the trailer brakes.

Combination Vehicles

All air tanks should be drained daily by opening their drain valves, even if they have automatic drains. Maintaining clean tanks helps to ensure that brakes will work correctly.

Shut-Off Valves

A trailer designed to connect with another trailer has shut-off valves (or cut-out cocks) on the service and emergency air lines. When multiple trailers are connected, all shut-off valves should be open to allow airflow between them. Only the valves on the last trailer should be closed. Similarly, when another trailer is not connected, the valves should be used to close off unused air lines.

Trailer Service, Parking, and Emergency Brakes

Although trailers built since 1975 have spring brakes, older converter dollies and trailers may not. They are, however, required to have emergency brakes. The emergency brake will come on when there is a significant air loss in the emergency line. It can also be manually engaged by pulling out the air supply knob. The emergency brake is controlled by air in the trailer air tank and will only stay engaged as long as there is enough air pressure in that tank.

Trailers without spring brakes lack parking brakes. Since the air that engages the emergency brakes may eventually leak out, causing them to fail, emergency brakes should not be relied on as a parking brake. Instead, in trailers without spring brakes, you must chock trailer wheels when parked.

Antilock Brake Systems

Trailers Required to Have ABS

An antilock brake system (ABS) reduces skidding while stopping, which allows greater steering control during hard braking. ABS, a brake accessory added to the standard air brake system, is required on trailers and converter dollies built on or after March 1, 1988. Dollies built after that date have a required yellow ABS malfunction light on their left side. ABS lights can also be found on the left front or rear corners of trailers.

TESTING ABS SYSTEMS

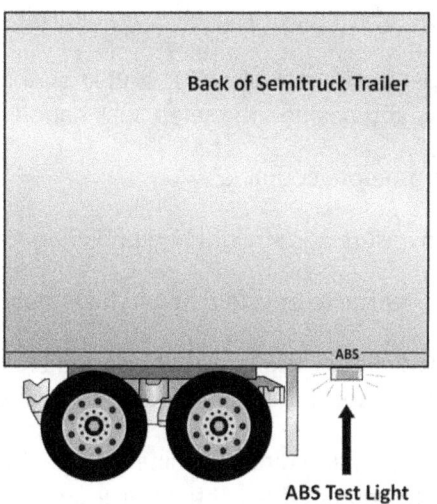

Combination Vehicles

Many vehicles built prior to the ABS requirement date have been retrofitted with ABS, though it may not be apparent without examining the brakes to see if they have electronic control unit (ECU) and wheel speed sensor wires coming from them. The sensors detect when the wheels might lock up, and the ECU tracks the sensors and controls the valves to engage the brake when necessary. You will also notice an electrical line running along the air line in trailers with ABS.

It is important to note whether one part of your combination vehicle (tractor, trailer, dolly) has ABS while another doesn't. If, for example, you rely on the ABS in your tractor when braking hard, the wheels of an attached trailer without ABS could lock up and skid, potentially causing a jackknife.

Braking with ABS

Driving a combination vehicle equipped with ABS does not enhance your ability to brake more quickly, nor should it impact the way you brake. As always, aim for slow, careful braking, frequently checking your mirrors to detect any trailer sway or loss of control. ABS does not allow you to stop in a shorter distance; it only allows you to better steer and control the vehicle when braking.

Should hard braking be necessary in a combination vehicle with ABS brakes, push down on the brake pedal and hold it down. The ABS computer regulates pressure applied to the brakes, preventing wheel lock up and allowing you to maintain better control of your vehicle. ABS on even a single trailer axle can help prevent trailer swing and jackknifing caused by wheels locking up. However, even with ABS, should the trailer start to sway, ease off the brakes. Should your ABS system fail, prompt service is recommended, but that will not affect your normal braking system.

Coupling and Uncoupling

Being able to couple and uncouple parts of a combination vehicle is essential to safe operation. Though different set-ups may require specific knowledge, this section provides general steps for coupling and uncoupling combination rigs.

Coupling Tractor-Semitrailers

1. Check the fifth wheel and all its parts to ensure that they are present and undamaged, and that all fasteners are tight. The fifth wheel must be securely mounted on the tractor and adequately greased. Driving a rig without enough grease between the upper (trailer) fifth wheel and lower (tractor or dolly) fifth wheel parts could cause friction, which may make steering difficult.

The fifth wheel must be in the proper position to allow for coupling. Angle the skid plate down toward the tractor's rear. Open the locking jaws and position the safety lock handle for automatic locking.

Sliding fifth wheels should be locked before coupling.

Inspect the kingpin on the trailer to ensure it is straight and undamaged.

2. Inspect the area surrounding the vehicle to ensure that you have clearance for coupling.

Secure the trailer by chocking the wheels or making sure the spring brakes are on. Inspect the cargo and secure as necessary to make sure it will not shift when the tractor is coupled to the trailer.

3. Position the tractor so that it is straight and directly in line with the front of the trailer. From outside your cab, visually check to see that the outer edges of the trailer are in line with the outer edges of the tractor's outermost tires or mudflaps. Backing under a trailer at an angle could either push the trailer out of position or damage its front supports (landing gear).

Combination Vehicles

Use both side mirrors to monitor your position as you align with the trailer.

4. Back up your tractor slowly and avoid hitting the trailer. Stop when the truck's skid plate first contacts the trailer apron.

5. For safety, put the tractor in neutral and apply the parking brake. Step out of the truck to inspect the alignment of the tractor and trailer.

6. Adjust the trailer height as necessary so that the tractor raises the trailer when backed into position. Having the trailer at the wrong height when you back up your tractor could cause damage to the trailer nose (if too low) or prevent proper coupling (if too high).

Visually confirm that the trailer kingpin is lined up with the tractor fifth wheel (skid plate) so that they will fit together for proper coupling.

7. Prepare to connect the emergency air line from the tractor to the trailer. Check that the glad hand seals are intact and clean before connecting. Secure air lines in a location where they won't be damaged or caught during coupling.

8. Send air to the tractor by either pushing in the "trailer air supply" knob or switching the tractor protection valve control to "normal." Once the air pressure is normal, turn off the engine and test the brakes to ensure that your emergency and service air lines are not crossed.

Listen for the sound to the trailer brakes moving as you apply them and the sound of air escaping when you release them.

If the air pressure gauge indicates that there has been no significant air loss, and brakes are functioning, then restart the engine. Check to ensure that air pressure stays normal.

9. Lock the trailer brakes by either pulling out the "trailer air supply" knob or returning the tractor protection valve control to "emergency."

10. In the lowest reverse gear, slowly back up the tractor until the lockjaw of the tractor's fifth wheel clasps onto the trailer's kingpin.

11. Crank landing gear up until just off the ground. With trailer brakes still engaged, slowly and gently pull the tractor forward, tugging on the trailer to ensure that it is securely in the fifth wheel.

12. So that you may safely inspect underneath the truck, put the tractor in neutral, apply the parking brakes, turn off the engine, and remove the key.

13. Inspect the coupling of the upper and lower fifth wheel; there should be no visible space between them. If there is visible space, the locking jaws of the lower fifth wheel have likely not correctly engaged with the kingpin.

Look under the fifth wheel from the back to the ensure that the locking jaws are around the kingpin shank. Appy the locking lever safety or ensure that it has been applied automatically.

Do not drive a rig with improper coupling. The trailer is at risk of coming loose from the tractor.

Combination Vehicles

14. Connect the electrical cord to the trailer and apply its safety. Inspect air lines and electrical lines for damage and store them in a way that prevents them from rubbing or coming into contact with moving vehicle parts.

15. First raise the landing gear in a low gear range if available before switching to a high gear range once the supports are no longer bearing weight. Crank until the landing gear has been completely raised and secure the crank handle.

Once the trailer is bearing the full weight of the tractor, check to make sure that there is enough clearance to prevent the tractor frame from hitting the landing gear while turning. Also ensure that there is enough space between the tractor tires and the trailer nose.

16. Remove and store trailer wheel chocks.

Uncoupling Tractor-Semitrailers

1. Line up the tractor in a straight line with the trailer to avoid damaging landing gear. Before uncoupling, ensure that the parking surface will support the trailer's weight.

2. Lock the trailer brakes by pulling out the air supply or switching the tractor protection valve to "emergency."

Gently back up tractor. With less pressure on the locking jaws, it will be easier to release the fifth wheel safety lock lever.

Apply the tractor parking brake to hold it in place while the front of the lower fifth wheel is pushing against the kingpin (decreasing pressure on the locking jaws).

3. In trailers that don't or may not have spring brakes, chock the wheels to avoid the trailer moving if the air tank loses pressure.

4. Lower the landing gear until firmly planted on the ground. For a loaded trailer, continue to turn the crank in a low gear a few extra turns beyond when the supports contact the ground. By doing this to take some of the trailer's weight off the tractor, the fifth wheel will be easier to release, and the trailer will be easier to couple again.

5. Disconnect air and electrical lines from the trailer. Keep glad hands clean by coupling them to dummy couplers or each other. Keep the electrical plug dry by hanging it plug-down. Store lines appropriately to avoid rubbing or contact with moving parts that might damage them.

6. Use the release handle lock to unlock the fifth wheel. Raise the handle and pull it to the "open" position. Be careful to avoid the rear tractor wheels when releasing the fifth wheel in case they move upon release.

7. Slowly drive tractor forward. As a safeguard against a failure in the landing gear, stop when the fifth wheel is out from under the trailer, but the tractor frame is still under the trailer.

8. Put the tractor in neutral and engage the parking brake.

9. Visually inspect the landing gear to make sure it is undamaged and that the trailer is adequately supported by the ground.

10. Release the tractor parking brake and pull forward until the tractor is clear of the trailer.

Combination Vehicles

Coupling a Pintle Hook

1. Check that the pintle hook is undamaged, securely mounted, and has all parts present. An unsecure pintle hook could allow the trailer to separate, causing serious damage, injury, or even death.

2. Remove the tethered wire, open the lock pin, and pull the lock handle away from the lock seat. Swing open the latch assembly upward as far as it will go, and then release. These steps are shown in the images below.

Locked Pintle Hook

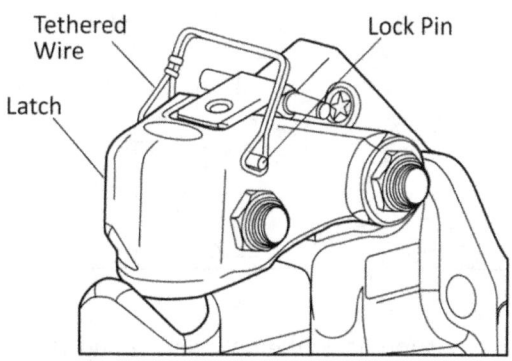

Pintle Hook Parts

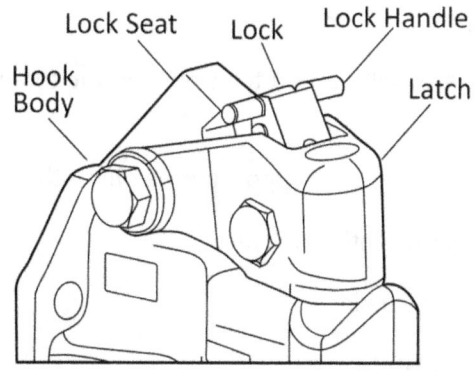

Open Pintle Hook

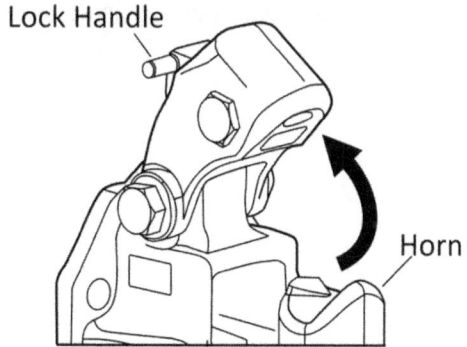

3. Lower the dolly drawbar into the horn of the pintle hook.

Combination Vehicles

4. Close the latch and be sure that the lock handle is flush with the top of the latch, indicating it is locked, as shown below. Reinsert the lock pin and put the tethered wire on. An unsecure latch could allow the trailer to separate.

Closing the Pintle Hook

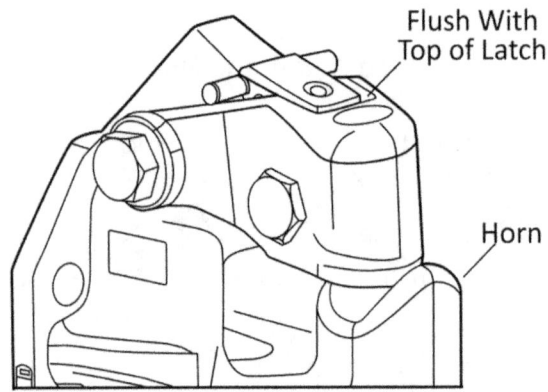

Uncoupling a Pintle Hook

1. Park on an even surface capable of supporting the rig's weight and chock the trailer tires.

2. Disconnect the safety chains, electrical line, and breakaway switch.

3. Unlock and then open the coupler.

4. Be sure the surface below the trailer will support the weight of the tongue (the part of the trailer that connects to the pintle hook).

5. Adjust the jack to the appropriate height to support the weight of the trailer tongue.

6. Lift the trailer coupler away from the pintle hook hitch.

7. Move the tow vehicle away from the trailer.

Inspecting a Combination Vehicle

Combination vehicles have more parts to inspect than single vehicles, though their inspection should also include the steps previously described for a general inspection. In addition, complete the checks described below.

Combination Vehicles

Additional Things to Check During a Walk-Around Inspection
Coupling System Areas
The fifth wheel is where the trailer couples with the tractor (or dolly). The upper fifth wheel, or trailer apron, is a metal plate around the kingpin, which fits into the locking jaws of the lower fifth wheel, the skid plate on the tractor.

Lower and Upper Fifth Wheels for Coupling

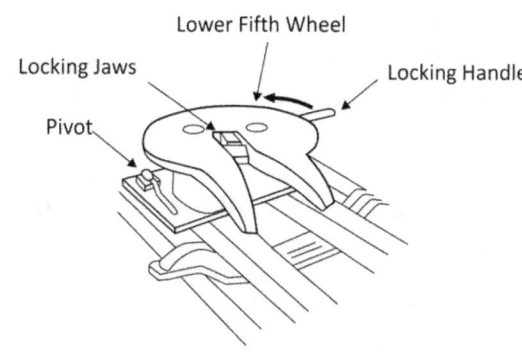

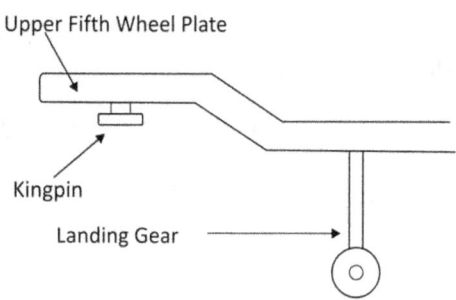

Coupled Lower and Upper Fifth Wheels

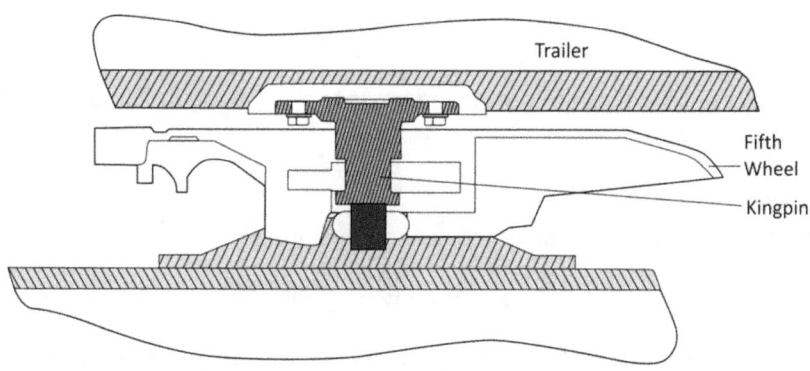

When inspecting, check all areas of the coupling system (fifth wheel) to ensure that there are no missing parts or signs of serious rust or damage, including buckling, cracks, chips, or welding defects. Check to ensure that all necessary bolts and pins are there, appropriately tightened, and undamaged.

Check that the lower fifth wheel platform (under the skid plate) is intact, undamaged, and securely attached to the tractor frame.

Check that the upper fifth wheel is undamaged and securely attached to the trailer frame.

Check that the kingpin is straight and undamaged.

Ensure that both the tractor skid plate and the trailer apron are well greased to prevent friction-caused steering problems. Check that the fifth wheel coupler (locking) jaws rest on the kingpin shank because locking jaws around the kingpin head are not secure. Visually check that the trailer apron is flat on the skid plate; there should be no space between the two.

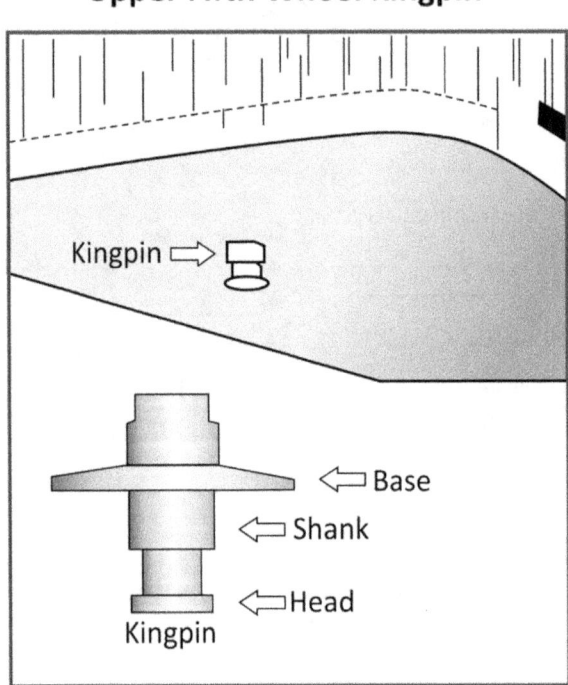

Upper Fifth Wheel Kingpin

Once the upper and lower fifth wheel are connected, engage the release (locking) handle in the locked position and apply the safety lock.

Air and Electric Lines
Check lines for damage including leaks, splits, cuts, and swelling.

Lines should be secured so they do not rub against anything, which could cause damage.

Ensure air and electric lines are connected to the trailer without leaking. Check glad hands to be sure that their gaskets are intact and they are properly connected with slack to allow for stretching during turns.

Electrical prongs should be clean and plugged in completely on both ends (tractor and trailer).

Combination Vehicles

Sliding Fifth Wheel
The skid plate of a sliding fifth wheel moves along a track to adjust the space between tractor and trailer. Below are additional checks for a sliding fifth wheel.

Inspect the slide to be sure that all parts are there and undamaged. It should be adequately greased.

Check for leaks in air-powered slides.

Ensure that all locking pins are present, undamaged, and completely locked into the grooves in the track.

Check fifth wheel position: be sure that there is enough room while turning to prevent the tractor from coming into contact with the landing gear or the trailer.

Sliding Fifth Wheel

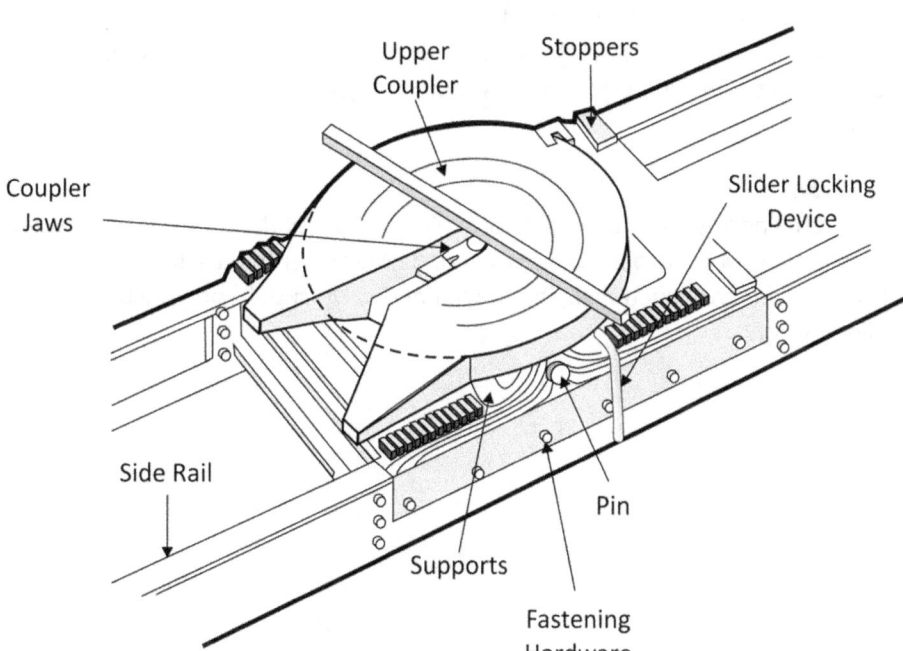

Landing Gear
Check the landing gear for damage.

Before driving, the landing gear should be completely raised with crank handle secured.

Check for leaks in air-powered or hydraulic-powered landing gear.

Combination Vehicle Brake Check
Check That Air Flows to All Trailers
Stabilize the vehicle with the tractor parking brake and/or wheel chocks. Once the gauge indicates that air pressure is normal, push the "trailer air supply" knob or turn the valve to "normal" to send air to the emergency air lines. Supply air to the service air line using the trailer handbrake. At the rear of the last trailer, open the emergency line shut-off valve and listen. The sound of air escaping indicates that all

Combination Vehicles

vehicles in the combination system are appropriately charged. Next, with the trailer hand brake still on or the brake foot pedal applied, close the emergency air line valve and open the service air line valve. Listen to ensure that the service air travels to the end of the rearmost trailer, and then close the valve. Only if you hear air coming from both lines can you be sure that the brakes work. If you do not hear the air from both lines, check that the other trailer and dolly shut-off valves are open.

Test the Tractor Protection Valve
Press the "trailer air supply" knob on the dash or turn the valve to "normal" to charge the trailer brake system with air pressure. Turn off the engine and repeatedly press the foot brake to release air from the storage tanks. When the pressure falls to between 20 and 45 psi, the "trailer air supply" knob will pop out (or the valve will turn to "emergency"). If that doesn't happen, the tractor protection valve isn't working properly. Without this safeguard, a leak could deplete trailer air tanks and cause the trailer emergency brakes to engage while driving, possibly causing a loss of control.

Test Trailer Emergency Brakes
Press the "trailer air supply" knob on the dash or turn the valve to "normal" to charge the trailer brake system with air pressure. The trailer should move easily. Then pull the "trailer air supply" knob or turn the valve to "emergency." The trailer emergency brakes should engage. Gently move forward with the tractor to verify that trailer brakes are active.

Test Trailer Service Brakes
Check the gauge to verify normal air pressure before releasing the parking brake. While slowly moving forward, use the trailer hand valve (trolley valve) to engage the trailer brakes. If the trailer brakes engage, they are properly connected and functional. The trailer hand valve should only be used for testing the brakes, never while driving.

Practice Quiz

1. To keep your combination vehicle from rolling over, you should:
    a. Keep cargo low in the center of the trailer and slow down around turns.
    b. Keep cargo low in the center of the trailer and speed up around turns.
    c. Stack cargo as high as possible in the center of the trailer and slow down around turns.
    d. Stack cargo as high as possible in the center of the trailer and speed up around turns.

2. What is the best way to avoid a jackknife when your trailer is swinging while braking?
    a. Press firmly on the foot brake.
    b. Pump the foot brake to engage ABS.
    c. Release the brakes.
    d. Use the trailer hand valve.

3. Which statement about off-tracking is FALSE?
    a. Off-tracking can be dangerous for pedestrians.
    b. Off-tracking is when rear wheels follow a different path than front wheels.
    c. Longer vehicles off-track more than shorter vehicles.
    d. You should correct for off-tracking by swinging wide before turning.

4. Ideally, how should you back on a curved path?
    a. Back the trailer toward the driver side by first turning the steering wheel to the left.
    b. Back the trailer toward the driver side by first turning the steering wheel to the right.
    c. Back the trailer toward the passenger side by first turning the steering wheel to the left.
    d. Back the trailer toward the passenger side by first turning the steering wheel to the right.

5. What should you use the trailer hand valve for?
    a. To keep a trailer without spring brakes in park
    b. To prevent a swaying trailer from jackknifing
    c. To stop the trailer while driving
    d. To test the trailer brakes before driving

Answer Explanations

1. A: Choice *A* is correct because balancing cargo in the center of the trailer and keeping it low helps to keep the trailer's center of gravity lower, making it less likely to roll. Going slowly when turning or changing directions also reduces the risk of rollover. Choice *B* is incorrect because even if cargo is well positioned, combination vehicles are more likely to roll over if turns are taken at high speeds. Choice *C* is incorrect because while slowing down around turns will help prevent rollover, stacking cargo high in the trailer brings its center of gravity closer to the top, making it more likely to tip. Choice *D* is incorrect because stacking cargo high and speeding up around turns are both more likely to cause a trailer to roll over.

2. C: Choice *C* is correct because trailer swing happens when trailer brakes lock up and the wheels start skidding. Releasing the brake stops the skid and allows you to regain control with gentle steering. Choice *A* is incorrect because braking is what is causing the skid and the swaying; continuing to brake will not fix it. Choice *B* is incorrect because pumping the brake is unnecessary with ABS brakes; the brakes regulate themselves when you apply and hold them. Choice *D* is incorrect because you should never use the trailer hand valve when driving; it will cause the emergency trailer brakes to engage, which will further cause the trailer to skid and swing.

3. D: Choice *D* is correct because you should correct for off-tracking by swinging wide *while* turning, not *before* turning. If you swing wide before turning, other drivers may pass you on the side. Choice *A* is incorrect because it is true; off-tracking can be dangerous for pedestrians if part of a truck travels over a sidewalk. Choice *B* is incorrect because it is the definition of off-tracking: when the rear wheels follow a different path than the front wheels. Choice *C* is incorrect because it is true; longer vehicles off-track more than shorter vehicles.

4. B: Choice *B* is correct because it's easier to back the trailer to the driver's side so that you can see the trailer more clearly in your mirror and out of your window while backing up. In a combination vehicle, you must first start backing up with the wheel turned in the direction opposite from the way you want the trailer to turn; therefore, for the trailer to turn toward the driver side, you must turn the steering wheel toward the passenger side (to the right). Choice *A* is incorrect because while you do want to back the trailer toward the driver side, turning the steering wheel to the left will turn the trailer toward the passenger side. Choices *C* and *D* are incorrect because it's easier to back the trailer toward the driver side so you can see better.

5. D: Choice *D* is correct because the trailer hand valve should be used only to test the trailer brakes before driving. Choice *A* is incorrect because trailers without spring brakes have no emergency brakes. If the trailer hand valve is used to supply air to the trailer brakes in park, and the air in the system leaks out, the trailer will have no brakes and may start moving. Choice *B* is incorrect because trailers sway and jackknife when the wheels lock up and skid due to braking; using the trailer hand valve to apply the trailer brake will only contribute to the problem. Choice *C* is incorrect because the trailer hand valve should never be used when driving. Instead, the service brakes should be used because they apply brakes to the entire vehicle, while the trailer hand valve only operates the trailer's brakes. Applying only the trailer's brakes while moving could cause a loss of control.

Doubles and Triples

Pulling Double/Triple Trailers

Driving a rig with double and triple trailers requires extra precautions. A longer vehicle with more parts and connections comes with less vehicle stability and more opportunities for safety issues. This section discusses those unique situations.

Complete Inspection
Each additional trailer in a combination vehicle system adds more parts and connections, which increases the risk for error or malfunction. Conduct a thorough inspection of your double and triple trailer combination vehicle according to the steps outlined in the section "Inspecting Doubles and Triples."

Preventing Trailer Rollover
It is especially important when pulling double and triple trailers to steer gently and decrease speed when changing directions. When driving around curves, turning corners, and taking on-ramps and off-ramps while towing two or three trailers, you may need to slow down considerably more than you would when driving a straight truck or single trailer in similar circumstances.

The Crack-the-Whip Effect
Double and triple trailer rigs are much less stable than straight trucks and single trailers. They require particularly gentle steering to help avoid dangerous sideways trailer movement. Doubles and triples are more likely to experience the crack-the-whip effect that commonly causes rollover, with the rearmost trailer being the most likely to roll over.

Looking Far Ahead
Looking ahead is important when operating any vehicle, especially when driving doubles and triples. Their increased length and instability create an increased risk of rollover or jackknife, particularly while braking hard or changing directions quickly. Looking ahead while driving gives you more reaction time and allows you to adjust for any issues ahead with cautious lane changes or slow, careful braking, both of which reduce the likelihood of rollover or a jackknife.

Managing Space
In addition to being longer, doubles and triples require more space to stop, change lanes, and turn. Leave more following distance between your truck and vehicles ahead in order to allow enough distance to stop carefully without having to apply sudden, hard pressure to the brake pedal. That will help prevent the wheels from locking up and possibly causing loss of control. Change lanes cautiously, and only after being sure you have enough space for your entire vehicle and time to steer gently into the lane without a sudden change in direction. When turning into or crossing traffic, be sure there is enough space for you to make the turn at a reasonable speed to reduce the risk of rollover.

Adverse Conditions
In addition to being longer, double and triple trailer combination vehicles have more dead axles. Because dead axles are only weight-bearing and do not provide power to the wheels they support, the powered axles on the vehicle must pull them. The greater number of dead axles increases the risk for loss of wheel traction, which could result in skidding, trailer sway, and jackknifing. Driving through the mountains, in bad weather, on slippery roads, or in other adverse conditions increases this risk even more. Driving doubles and triples in such adverse conditions requires extra caution and care.

Parking the Vehicle
The easiest way to park a combination vehicle with double or triple trailers is to do so in such a way that you can pull forward trough the parking spot. Always be aware of where you are parking and aim to park in a pull-through spot. Backing out of a parking spot with a multi-trailer rig can be extremely difficult and time consuming.

Antilock Braking Systems on Converter Dollies
Antilock brake systems (ABS), a brake accessory added to the standard air brake system, are required on trailers and converter dollies built on or after March 1, 1988. Dollies built after that date have a required yellow ABS malfunction light on their left side. Many dollies built prior to the requirement date have been retrofitted with ABS systems.

Coupling and Uncoupling

This section describes the steps for safe coupling and uncoupling in twin and triple tailers. Being able to safely couple and uncouple is essential for safely operating combination vehicles with multiple trailers.

Coupling Twin Trailers
First, decide how to arrange the trailers appropriately. Doubles are easier to handle when the heaviest trailer is coupled behind the tractor, and the lightest trailer is behind that (in the rear).

Secure Second Trailer
Before coupling, secure the brakes on the rearmost trailer. If the trailer does not have spring brakes or you are unsure, chock the wheels as a precaution.

If the trailer does not have spring brakes, back the tractor near the trailer and hook up the emergency line to the trailer. Be sure the shut-off valves on the trailer are closed so it will maintain air. To engage the trailer's emergency brakes, fill the trailer air tank before disconnecting the emergency line. Brakes will only engage if the slack adjusters are set, as necessary, to compensate for any brake pad wear.

A converter dolly provides the axles needed to support the front end of the rear trailer and couple it with the tractor-trailer, creating a twin trailer combination vehicle, as shown in the image below. A dolly has one or two axles and a fifth wheel that engages with the rear trailer's kingpin.

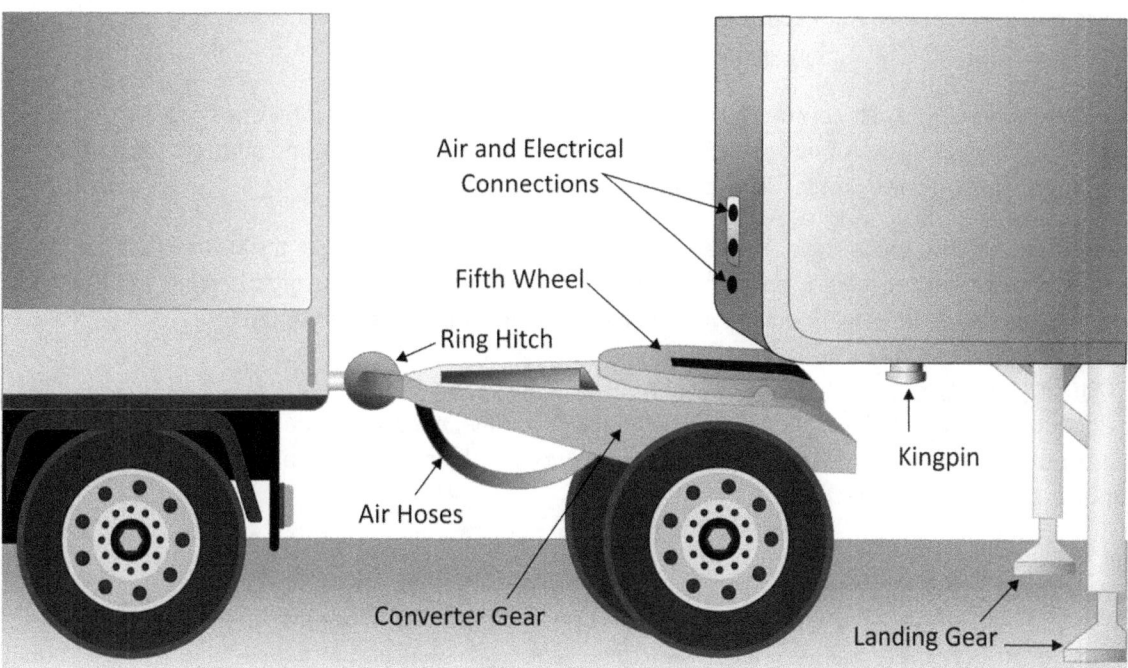

Position Converter Dolly
To begin coupling, release the dolly's brakes and move it into place. Open the petcock valve to release air from the dolly's air tanks or, in the case of spring brakes, release the dolly parking brake knob.

If possible, it may be easier to move the dolly into position by hand.

If necessary, pick up the converter dolly using the tractor-trailer combination. Move the tractor-trailer to the converter dolly and connect the dolly and trailer using the ring hitch. Lock the pintle hook. Fully raise the dolly support and secure it. Drive the combination so the dolly is close to the second trailer's nose, and then lower the dolly support and unhook it from the front trailer.

Before coupling, ensure that the dolly is centered to the second trailer and align its fifth wheel with the second trailer's kingpin. Position the dolly so that its fifth wheel is nearly touching the trailer nose.

Connect Converter Dolly to Front Trailer
Position the tractor-trailer combination in front of the converter dolly and connect the dolly to the lead trailer. Lock the pintle hook, attach safety chains, and connect the dolly's air and electrical lines. Fully raise the dolly's landing gear and secure it.

Connect Converter Dolly to Rear Trailer
Be sure that the rear trailer is secured (see "Secure Second Trailer" section above).

Use the landing gear crank to adjust the trailer's height so that it is just lower than the dolly's fifth wheel. The rear trailer should rise when the dolly is backed under it.

Back the tractor-trailer-dolly combination under the back trailer. Ensure that the rear trailer's landing gear is off the ground in case it moves when testing the connection. Pull the tractor forward slowly and gently to test the connection of the dolly and the rear trailer. Visually check the coupling from behind the fifth wheel to ensure that there is no space between the upper and lower fifth wheel and that the locking jaws are properly engaged on the kingpin shank.

Connect air hoses and electrical cord from the dolly to the second trailer. To fill the system with air, close the petcock on the dolly's air tank, and close the service and emergency air line shut-off valves on the rear trailer. Open shut-off valves on lead trailer and dolly, if present.

Raise the landing gear and secure the crank. Push "trailer air supply" knob on the dash to send air to the brakes. At the rear of the vehicle, open the second trailer's emergency line shut-off valve and listen for airflow. The brakes will not work unless you hear air coming from the system there.

Uncoupling Twin Trailers

First uncouple the rear trailer. Park the vehicle in a straight line, engage the parking brakes, and chock the wheels of the second trailer if it lacks spring brakes. Avoid parking in uneven areas or on surfaces unable to support the trailer's weight.

Lower the second trailer's landing gear to the ground until it lifts weight off the converter dolly.

Close the air shut-off valves on the front trailer and dolly, if present, before disconnecting the air and electric lines from the rear trailer. Release the converter dolly brakes and fifth wheel latch. Drive your tractor forward, slowly pulling the dolly away from the rear semitrailer.

Next, uncouple the converter dolly from the lead trailer: fully lower the landing gear, remove safety chains, and engage spring brakes (or chock wheels if no spring brakes are present). Only after uncoupling from the rear trailer, unlock the pintle hook to release the dolly from the front trailer. Releasing the pintle hook with the weight of the second trailer on the dolly is very dangerous; it could cause the dolly tow bar to swing up quickly. Minimally, it will make it difficult to position the dolly for recoupling with a front trailer.

Once the dolly is unattached and supported on its landing gear, slowly drive the tractor and first trailer away from the dolly.

Coupling and Uncoupling Triple Trailers

Begin by coupling your tractor to the first trailer. Couple the front trailer to the second trailer and that trailer to the third.

Uncouple by first removing the dolly from under the third trailer. Unhitch that dolly and uncouple the rest of the vehicle.

Coupling and Uncoupling Other Combinations

While this manual discusses coupling and uncoupling for common combination vehicles, there are many different types of combinations in use. Familiarize yourself with the manufacturer and/or owner specifications for your rig components to learn the appropriate steps for coupling and uncoupling.

Inspecting Doubles and Triples

Combination vehicles have more parts than single vehicles, and they also have some unique characteristics to inspect, which are described in this section.

Additional Checks

In addition to a standard inspection, double or triple combination vehicles should also be checked specifically for each of the following.

Coupling Area

Ensure that the lower fifth wheel is securely mounted and adequately greased with no missing or damaged parts.

From behind the fifth wheel, verify that there is no visible space between the upper and lower parts.

Be sure that the skid plate locking jaws are engaged on the kingpin shank and the release arm is secured.

Ensure that the glide plate of the upper fifth wheel is secure and the kingpin is undamaged.

Be sure air lines are securely connected to glad hands with no air leaking and the electrical cord is plugged in. Be sure all lines are undamaged and secured with slack for turns.

Ensure that the sliding fifth wheel is adequately greased without missing or damaged parts. Be sure all locking pins are present, undamaged, and locked into their grooves. Check for leaks in an air-powered slide. Check the position of the fifth wheel to be sure there is enough room while turning to prevent the tractor from coming into contact with the landing gear or the trailer.

Landing Gear

Check that landing gear is undamaged and all parts are present. Supports should be fully raised with the crank handle secured. Check for air or hydraulic leaks in power-operated landing gear.

Double and Triple Trailers

Service and emergency line shut-off valves should be open on the front and middle trailers and closed on the last trailer. The petcock valve on the dollies' air tanks should be closed. All air lines should be properly connected at the glad hands without leaks, and they should be secured to avoid rubbing or other damage. Light cords should be firmly plugged in.

If present, the spare tire on the dolly should be secured. The dolly's pintle-eye should be securely in the trailer's pintle hook, which should be latched. Check that the dolly's safety chains are connected to the trailer(s).

Doubles/Triples Air Brake Check

Check the brakes on a double or triple trailer as previously described and as described below.

Additional Air Brake Checks

Stabilize the Vehicle

Stabilize the vehicle with the tractor parking brake and/or wheel chocks. Once the gauge indicates that air pressure is normal, push the "trailer air supply" knob or turn valve to "normal" to send air to the emergency air lines. Supply air to the service air line by using the trailer handbrake. At the rear of the last

trailer, open the emergency line shut-off valve and listen. The sound of air escaping indicates that all vehicles in the combination system are appropriately charged. Next, with the trailer hand brake still on or the brake foot pedal applied, close the emergency air line valve and open the service air line valve. Listen to ensure that the service air travels to the end of the rearmost trailer, and then close the valve. Only if you hear air coming from both lines can you be sure that the brakes will work. If you do not hear the air from both lines, check the front and middle trailer and dolly shut-off valves to ensure that they are open.

Test Tractor Protection Valve
Press the "trailer air supply" knob on the dash or turn the valve to "normal" to charge the trailer brake system with air pressure. Turn off the engine and press the foot brake a few times to release air from the storage tanks. When the pressure falls to between 20 and 45 psi, the "trailer air supply" knob will pop out (or the valve will turn to "emergency"). If that doesn't happen, the tractor protection valve isn't working properly. Without this safeguard, a leak could deplete trailer air tanks and cause the trailer emergency brakes to engage while driving, locking up the wheels and possibly causing a loss of control.

Test Trailer Emergency Brakes
Press the "trailer air supply" knob on the dash or turn the valve to "normal" to charge the trailer brake system with air pressure. The trailer should move easily. Then pull the "trailer air supply" knob or turn the valve to "emergency." The trailer emergency brakes should engage. Gently move forward with the tractor to verify that the trailer brakes are active.

Test Trailer Service Brakes
Check the gauge to verify normal air pressure before releasing the parking brake. While slowly moving forward, use the trailer hand valve (trolley valve) to engage the trailer brakes. If the trailer brakes engage, then they are properly connected and functional. The trailer hand valve should only be used for testing the brakes, never while driving.

Practice Quiz

1. Why are double and triple trailer vehicles more likely to skid?
    a. They have more dead axles.
    b. They have more fifth wheel connections.
    c. They are more likely to be coupled incorrectly.
    d. They are more likely to experience the crack-the-whip effect.

2. Which statement about converter dollies is true?
    a. All converter dollies have ABS.
    b. All converter dollies have spring brakes.
    c. Converter dollies connect tractor-trailers with semitrailers.
    d. Converter dollies always have a single wheel axle.

3. Which shows the correct order for coupling a semitrailer to a tractor-trailer combination?
    a. Position the converter dolly, secure the second trailer, connect the dolly to the front trailer, and then connect the dolly to the rear trailer.
    b. Position the converter dolly, secure the second trailer, connect the dolly to the rear trailer, and then connect the dolly to the front trailer.
    c. Secure the second trailer, position the converter dolly, connect the dolly to the front trailer, and then connect the dolly to the rear trailer.
    d. Secure the second trailer, position the converter dolly, connect the dolly to the rear trailer, and then connect the dolly to the front trailer.

4. What is the correct height of the second trailer before coupling with the converter dolly?
    a. The second trailer is much lower than the dolly's fifth wheel.
    b. The second trailer is slightly higher than the dolly's fifth wheel.
    c. The second trailer is slightly lower than the dolly's fifth wheel.
    d. The second trailer is at the same height as the dolly's fifth wheel.

5. Which of the following indicates a good connection between the converter dolly and the rear trailer?
    a. The connection holds when the tractor is pulled forward slightly.
    b. The dolly pulls away from the trailer when the tractor is pulled forward.
    c. The locking jaws of the fifth wheel are on the head of the kingpin.
    d. There is visible space between the upper and lower fifth wheel.

Answer Explanations

1. A: Choice *A* is correct because doubles and triples have more dead, or unpowered, axles, making them more likely to skid. Choice *B* is incorrect because the fifth wheel connections do not affect the wheels or skidding. Choice *C* is incorrect because incorrect coupling is not related to skidding. Choice *D* is incorrect because skidding causes the crack-the-whip effect, not the other way around.

2. C: Choice *C* is correct because a converter dolly connects two trailers in a double or triple combination vehicle. Choice *A* is incorrect because dollies manufactured before March 1, 1988, may not have ABS. Choice *B* is incorrect because not all dollies have spring brakes. Choice *D* is incorrect because some dollies have two-wheel axles.

3. C: Choice *C* is correct because this is the order in which you should connect a semitrailer to a tractor-trailer combination. Choice *A* is incorrect because the second trailer should be secured first. Choice *B* is incorrect because the second trailer should be secured first, and the dolly should connect to the front trailer before being connected to the rear trailer. Choice *D* is incorrect because the dolly should connect to the front trailer before being connected to the rear trailer.

4. C: Choice *C* is correct because the trailer height should be just lower than the dolly's fifth wheel so that the rear trailer rises when the dolly is backed under it. Choice *A* is incorrect because if the second trailer is too low, the dolly may hit the trailer nose and damage it. Choice *B* is incorrect because if the trailer is higher than the dolly's fifth wheel, the locking jaws won't be able to engage with the shank of the kingpin, or there may be space between the upper and lower fifth wheels. Choice *C* is incorrect because if the second trailer is too low, the dolly may hit and damage the trailer nose. Choice *D* is incorrect because the fifth wheels may not connect properly if the second trailer is not slightly lower than the dolly's fifth wheel.

5. A: Choice *A* is correct because, in addition to a visual inspection, pulling the tractor forward gently is a good way to test the connection between the dolly and the rear trailer. Choice *B* is incorrect because a good connection should not be easily broken; otherwise, the trailer may come loose during operation. Choice *C* is incorrect because the locking jaws of the fifth wheel should rest on the shank of the kingpin, not the head. Choice *D* is incorrect because there should be no visible space between the upper and lower fifth wheels when they're properly coupled.

Tank Vehicles

This section provides information necessary to pass the CDL knowledge test for tank vehicles that transport liquids or gases. In vehicles that require a Class A or Class B CDL, the tank endorsement is necessary when driving vehicles with permanently or temporarily mounted tank(s) with individual rated capacity of greater than 119 gallons and an aggregate rated capacity of at least 1,000 gallons.

Inspecting Tank Vehicles

Tank vehicles have unique features that must be inspected before loading, unloading, or driving. There are many kinds of tank vehicles; refer to your vehicle's operator manual to ensure that you inspect all parts relevant to the model you are operating.

Leaks

Every tank vehicle must be inspected for leaks. Operating a leaking tank vehicle is a criminal offense that will result in a citation. If cited, you will be prohibited from driving further and may be responsible for spill clean-up.

Before loading or unloading, always check the positioning of the intake, discharge, and cut-off valves. Make sure that manholes are covered and valves are closed before driving.

Ensure that the tank's body and shell are free from dents or leaks and that there are no signs of leakage around or under your vehicle.

Inspect valves, pipes, and connections, particularly near joints where leaks are more likely.

Ensure that the manhole covers' gaskets are present and closed.

Makes sure that vents are clear and working properly.

Check Special Purpose Equipment
If present, the following should be checked for proper functioning:

- Vapor recovery kits
- Grounding and bonding cables
- Emergency shut-off systems
- Fire extinguisher

Special Equipment
Check your operator manual to ensure that you have all emergency equipment required for your vehicle and that it works.

Driving Tank Vehicles

A higher center of gravity and liquid surges mean that tank vehicles require special handling skills, as described below.

High Center of Gravity
The center of gravity is the point where an object's weight is concentrated. A tanker truck has a high center of gravity (as shown in the image below) because the load's weight is carried high relative to the

base (the wheels). A high center of gravity affects the vehicle's balance and makes it more likely to roll over. Tankers have been known to roll over on curves even while traveling the posted speed limit. It is especially important to maintain a slow speed when taking curves, on-ramps, and off-ramps.

Danger of Surge

Liquid moves in surges when the truck changes direction or stops, and that can make it difficult to maneuver the truck. When turning or taking a curve, side-to-side surges may cause rollover. Liquid surges in a forward-to-back motion when the truck is stopping and accelerating. When stopping, for example, the liquid continues to move forward (as shown below) and can give the truck enough momentum to move even with the brakes engaged, especially in slippery conditions. To avoid being propelled into dangerous situations, drivers must know how to handle vehicles at risk for surges.

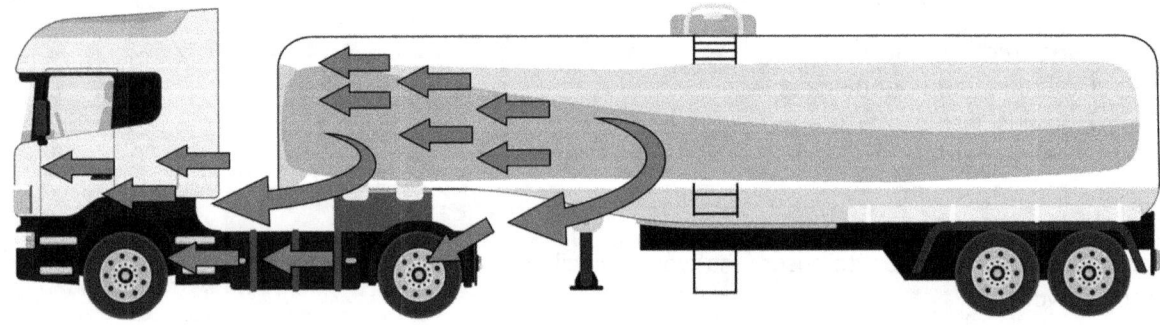

Bulkheads

Bulkheads are dividers that separate large tanks into several smaller compartments. With bulkheads, pay attention to even weight distribution; avoid putting extra weight in the front or rear of the tank.

Baffled Tanks

Baffled tanks also have separate compartments, but the baffles (dividers) have holes that allow flow between the compartments. Baffles help to reduce handling issues caused by liquid surging forward and backward in the tank. However, sideways surges are still possible.

Un-Baffled Tanks

Tanks without baffles, or smoothbore tanks, have no dividers to slow liquid or reduce surges. Front to back surges are common and strong in these tanks, so extreme caution is necessary, especially when stopping and accelerating.

Un-baffled tanks are commonly used to carry food products, like milk, because baffles make it difficult to adequately sanitize the tank.

Outage

Always leave space, or outage, in a tank for liquid cargo to expand as it warms. The amount of outage necessary varies by liquid. Know the outage required for the liquid you are hauling. Never completely fill a cargo tank.

How Much to Load?

In addition to the need for outage, some dense liquids may be too heavy to haul a tankful within legal weight limits. How full a tank is will depend on the following: how much the liquid expands, its weight, and the legal weight limits.

Safe Driving Rules

In addition to the driving rules previously discussed for combination vehicles, there are some special precautions to take when driving tank vehicles.

Drive Smoothly

Tankers' high center of gravity and liquid surges can make them difficult to handle, a problem made worse by abrupt changes in direction. Always drive smoothly, especially when accelerating, slowing down, stopping, turning, making lane changes, and taking curves, on-ramps, or off-ramps,

Controlling Surge

To control surge while braking, apply steady pressure to the brakes and hold for an extended time before releasing. To best ensure slow, smooth braking, increase following distance so you can anticipate the need to brake and allow for adequate braking distance. When a fast stop is necessary, use controlled or stab braking. Additionally, avoid quick steering maneuvers while braking to reduce the risk of rollover.

Curves

Slow smoothly before a curve and accelerate only slightly through the curve, staying below the posted speed limit. Driving at the posted speed limit through a curve could be fast enough to tip a tanker truck.

Stopping Distance

Allow adequate stopping distance, being aware of the need for smooth stops to control surge in loaded tank vehicles, while also being aware that empty tankers may require even more distance to stop than loaded ones. Road conditions impact stopping distance, with twice as much distance needed to stop a vehicle on wet roads.

Skids

Smooth driving is the key to avoiding skids. Steering, accelerating, or braking hard or abruptly can cause skids that may lead to a jackknife. Once you observe a skid, release the brakes to allow the wheels to regain traction and steer gently into the skid.

Practice Quiz

1. What is a safe speed for tank vehicles to drive on curves, on-ramps, and off-ramps?
    a. At the posted speed limit
    b. Below the posted speed limit
    c. No more than 6 mph above the posted speed limit
    d. At the same speed as you would drive a non-tanker trailer

2. Which statement about the types of tanker trucks is true?
    a. Baffles and bulkheads are two names for the same type of tanker.
    b. Baffles help to reduce handling issues due to surges.
    c. Bulkheads have holes in them that allow liquid to pass through.
    d. Smoothbore tanks are separated into compartments.

3. What factors affect the maximum amount of liquid loaded in a tank vehicle?
    a. How much the liquid will expand
    b. Legal weight limits
    c. The liquid's density
    d. All of the above

4. Which of the following is NOT a good way to control surge in a tank vehicle?
    a. Allow adequate stopping distance.
    b. Increase following distance.
    c. Make smooth lane changes.
    d. Pump the foot brake when stopping.

5. What two factors make tank vehicles require special handling compared with other combination vehicles?
    a. Center of gravity and surges
    b. Center of gravity and vehicle weight
    c. Surges and vehicle length
    d. Vehicle length and weight

Answer Explanations

1. B: Choice *B* is correct because tankers have been known to roll over on curves, even when traveling at the posted speed limit. It's safest to drive below the posted speed limit. For this reason, Choice *A* is incorrect. Choice *C* is incorrect because, to prevent rollover, you should not drive a tank vehicle above posted speed limit. Choice *D* is incorrect because tank vehicles are more likely to tip on curves than non-tankers, so you should take curves slower in tankers.

2. B: Choice *B* is correct because baffles separate a tank into smaller sections, which helps reduce the impact of liquid surge. Choice *A* is incorrect because baffles have holes in them that allow liquid to move through them, while bulkheads are dividers that separate individual tanks with no holes in them. Choice *C* is incorrect because bulkheads do not have holes in them, but baffles do. Choice *D* is incorrect because smoothbore tanks do not have any baffles or separators.

3. D: Choice *D* is correct because the amount of liquid loaded in a tank vehicle depends on all three factors listed: how much the liquid will expand, the legal weight limits, and the liquid's density. Choices *A*, *B*, and *C* are incorrect; while they are true when considered as individual propositions, none is the best answer because the other answers are true as well.

4. D: Choice *D* is correct because the proper way to stop a tank vehicle is to press the brake smoothly and hold it for an extended period of time to help control handling issues due to surge. Pumping the brake would only worsen the surge by making the liquid move more. The remaining choices are incorrect because they are good practices. Allowing adequate stopping distance and increasing following distance reduce the need to make sudden or harsh stops or turns that could cause surges. Making smooth lane changes also helps to reduce surges.

5. A: Choice *A* is correct because the high center of gravity and liquid surges in tank trucks can make them prone to rolling over and difficult to handle, respectively. Choice *B* is incorrect because it is less the vehicle's weight and more the shifting of the liquid's weight during driving that causes handling issues. Choice *C* is incorrect because surges do cause handling issues in tank trucks, but the vehicle length is not necessarily an issue. Choice *D* is incorrect because tank trucks' length and weight do not necessarily impact their handling as much as the center of gravity and liquid surges.

Hazardous Materials

Introduction to Hazardous Materials

As the operator of a CMV, transporting hazardous materials (also known as HAZMAT) may be a routine part of the job. The types of products commonly labeled as HAZMAT include gases, explosives, flammable and combustible liquids, oxidizing substances, flammable solids, poisons, corrosives, and radioactive substances. The federal government regulates the handling of these substances due to the danger that they pose if mishandled.

To read exactly what the federal government has to say regarding HAZMAT, refer to parts 171 to 180 of Title 49 Code of Federal Regulations (CFR), which is available online at www.ecfr.gov. The CFR provides a Hazardous Materials Table that lists many, but not all, hazardous substances. It's a good idea to review this table from time to time as a reminder of which materials pose risks. You can also refer to the U.S. Department of Transportation's website for a list of hazardous materials: www.transportation.gov.

Usually, the shipper decides whether a material meets the criteria for hazardous substances and will label them as such. Anyone transporting hazardous materials must display a diamond-shaped warning placard on their vehicle.

Regulations for transporting hazardous materials are frequently updated. It's your responsibility to be aware of these changes. Obtaining revised copies of the regulations and/or HAZMAT table is recommended. For your reference, the regulations contain a glossary defining all terms presented in them.

To transport HAZMAT, drivers must obtain a CDL that has a HAZMAT endorsement. Obtaining the endorsement requires you to take a written exam about hazardous material rules. It is recommended that you obtain a copy of the 49 CFR from your local union or Government Printing Office. You should also consider taking courses that focus on hazardous materials to reinforce your knowledge. These courses may be available in person or online. Check with local colleges and/or your employer for recommendations. The Pipeline and Hazardous Materials Safety Administration also sponsors training; you can contact them to ask about course availability. Their contact information is available on their website: www.phmsa.dot.gov.

Your employer or designated representative should provide training and testing to prepare you to transport hazardous materials, as required by HAZMAT regulations. The training should teach you how to respond to emergency situations involving the materials.

Different locations may require additional permits or special routes for carrying HAZMAT. There may also be some additional federal exemptions for certain products. Find out this information before you transport these items.

The Intent of Regulations

The purpose for the hazardous material regulations is to ensure the safety of the transporter and the public. They have three goals: to ensure that 1) the materials are contained properly, 2) shippers have communicated the risk involved in transporting them, and 3) the materials are transported safely by licensed drivers and with the right equipment.

Hazardous Materials

The regulations include containment rules. These rules tell shippers the safest ways to package hazardous materials. They inform transporters how to carry, load, and unload the products in the safest way possible.

Shippers are responsible for warning drivers and others about the risks involved with handling hazardous materials. They must properly label the products with warning labels and include any documentation that provides proper shipping instructions or emergency response instructions.

No one can transport hazardous materials without the appropriate licensure. They must pass a written exam about hazardous materials that covers everything, including how to identity the materials and safely load them, where to place placards, and how to transport the materials safely.

Always comply fully with regulations and do not take shortcuts. If you break the rules, you could be fined or sentenced to jail time. Just in case you are stopped by law enforcement, always inspect the shipment before, during, and after each trip.

Hazardous Materials Transportation—Who Does What?

The transport of hazardous materials involves three key roles: the shipper, the carrier, and the driver. Each have a specific set of responsibilities that help hazardous materials arrive safely to their destination.

The shipper sends the materials from point A to point B. The products may travel via vessel, truck, rail, or airplane. Shippers make sure that the products are labeled properly and have identification numbers, hazard class identification, warning labels, the right shipping name, and the correct packaging. They package and label the materials before transport, and they ensure that the proper documentation is included. The shipper must also indicate on shipping papers that products have been prepared in accordance with HAZMAT regulations.

A carrier retrieves the shipment from the shipper and takes it to the location where it will be picked up by the driver or transporter. Their role is to ensure that the shipper packaged the shipment properly. If preparation protocols have not been followed, the carrier must refuse the shipment. If any accidents occur involving the hazardous material, the carrier must report them to the government.

The driver double checks the shipments to make sure that the shipper properly packaged and labeled them. They look for anything that the shipper or carrier might have missed, like identification numbers and hazard class information. If the shipment has been damaged or there are leaks, the driver should refuse the shipment. The driver reviews the rules for transporting hazardous materials and collects the documentation that came with the materials. They will put any paperwork detailing how to handle an emergency in an easily accessible place.

Communication Rules

When it comes to handling hazardous materials, communication is key. From understanding the terminology used to describe the products to being able to understand the documentation that comes with them, everyone involved needs to know how to communicate effectively.

Definitions
Hazardous materials are organized into nine different hazard classes including explosives, flammable liquids, flammable solids, oxidizing substances, poisons, corrosives, flammable gases, radioactive substances, and miscellaneous substances.

Hazardous Materials

Hazardous Materials by Class			
Class	Division	Name of Class or Division	Examples
1	1.1	Mass explosives	Dynamite
	1.2	Projection hazards	Flares
	1.3	Mass fire hazards	Display fireworks
	1.4	Very insensitive	Ammunition
	1.5	Extreme insensitive	Blasting agents
			Explosive devices
2	2.1	Flammable gases	Propane
	2.2	Non-flammable gases	Helium
	2.3	Poisonous/toxic gases	Fluorine, compressed
3	-	Flammable liquids	Gasoline
4	4.1	Flammable gases	Ammonium picrate
	4.2	Spontaneously combustible	Wetted white
	4.3	Spontaneously combustible when wet	Phosphorus sodium
5	5.1	Oxidizers	Ammonium nitrate
	5.2	Organic peroxides	Methyl ethyl ketone
			Peroxide
6	6.1	Poison (toxic material)	Potassium cyanide
	6.2	Infectious substances	Anthrax virus
7	-	Radioactive	Uranium
8	-	Corrosives	Battery fluid
9	-	Miscellaneous Hazardous materials	Polychlorinated Biphenyls (PCB)
None	-	ORM-D (other regulated material-domestic)	Food flavorings, medicine
None	-	Combustible liquids	Fuel oil

As explained previously, the shipper, the carrier, and the driver/transporter all have distinct roles. Shippers must correctly identify hazardous materials on shipping paperwork. Shipping paperwork includes the identification of the materials being shipped, details about the order, the shipping manifest (which lists the crew, passengers, and cargo), and the bills of lading (which include details about the destination, quantity, and type of materials). Carriers and drivers need to understand this paperwork and keep it accessible and visible when transporting materials.

Types of Labels

Shippers place warning labels on shipments either as stickers or tags. These warning labels are usually diamond-shaped and brightly colored. The labels identify what kind of hazards items pose.

Placards are typically placed on the outside of vehicles or on bulk items. They identify the numerical hazard class of the shipment. Like package labels, placards are usually diamond shaped. Bulk packaging and cargo tanks display the identification numbers of hazardous materials on these placards. The identification number consists of four digits and can identify multiple substances. Keep a guide on hand like the Department of Transportation's Emergency Response Guidebook, which lists the different four-digit codes for hazardous materials.

Hazardous Materials Table

To identify hazardous materials, shippers refer to three sections of part 171 of the CFR: the Hazardous Materials Table in Section 171.101 and Appendices A and B. The table consists of 10 columns; however, only columns one through eight apply to transporting goods by driving. In a nutshell, the table provides the following information:

- Correct shipping names for hazardous materials
- The hazard class
- Shipping requirements

49 CFR 172.101 Hazardous Materials Table								
Symbols	Hazardous materials description and proper shipping names	Hazard class or division	Identification numbers	PG	Label Codes	Special provisions (172.102)	Packaging (173. ***)		
							Exceptions	Non bulk	Bulk
(1)	(2)	(3)	(4)	(5)	(6)	(7)	(8A)	(8B)	(8C)
A	Acetaldehyde ammonia	9	UN1841	III	9	IB8, IP6	155	204	240
	Acetaldehyde oxime	3	UN2332	III	3	B1, IB3, T4, TP1	150	203	242

To see full table, visit www.ecfr.gov.

The eight columns that apply to shipping via driving are classified as follows:

I. **Symbols:** these symbols represent special shipping conditions. "+" means the material is risky for humans; "A" means restrictions applicable when shipping by air; "D" represents domestic transportation; "G" represents generic proper shipping name; "I" is for international transportation; and "W" means the material should be transported by water vessel.
II. **Descriptions and proper shipping names:** this is where you find the correct names of the hazardous materials in alphabetical order. Proper shipping names should always be in normal font. Italicized names are not proper shipping names.
III. **Hazard class or division:** in addition to hazard classifications, this section will also tell you if a material is forbidden. The appropriate placards should be applied to hazardous shipments based on quantity and class number.
IV. **Identification numbers:** in front of every ID number are the letters NA, UN, or ID. "NA" identifies shipments that are transported between the United States and Canada. If "UN" precedes a code, it means it was codified by the United Nations Committee of Experts on the Transport of Dangerous Goods. Lastly, "ID" means that the shipment's name has been recognized by the International Civil Aviation Organization.
V. **Packaging group (PG):** a material's packaging group is represented by Roman numerals.
VI. **Label codes:** the class numbers that shippers put on packages to show what types of hazardous materials they contain
VII. **Special provisions:** additional requirements for handling hazardous materials
VIII. **Packaging:** the packaging requirements in column 8 are split into three specifications: exceptions, non-bulk, and bulk.

Hazardous Materials

| Appendix A: List of Hazardous Substances and Reportable Quantities ||
Hazardous Substances	Reportable Quantity (RQ) Pounds (Kilograms)
Phenyl mercaptan	100 (45.4)
Phenylmercury acetate	100 (45.4)
Phenylthiourea	100 (45.4)
Phorate	10 (4.54)
Phosgene	10 (4.54)
Phosphine	100 (45.4)
Phosphoric acid	5,000 (2270)
Phosphoric acid, diethyl4-nitrophenyl ester	100 (45.4)
Phosphoric acid, lead (2+) salt (2:3)	10 (.454)

If any hazardous substances spill during transport, the Department of Transportation and the Environmental Protection Agency need to know about it. The amount spilled must meet the reportable quantity (RQ) guidelines outlined in this appendix. This means that any spilled amount that is less than the RQ listed does not need to be reported. POISON INHALATION or POISON GAS placards must be displayed on any substance that poses an inhalation hazard, which should be noted in shipping paperwork.

| Appendix B: List of Marine Pollutants ||
Severe Marine Pollutant	Marine Pollutant
(1)	(2)
	Acetal
	Acetaldehyde
	Acetone cyanohydrin, stabilized
	Acetylene tetrabromide
	Acraldehyde, inhibited
	Acrolein, inhibited

Note: This is just a sample of the table. The full table is quite extensive.

In this appendix, you will find a list of substances that are hazardous to marine life. If transporting a container with 119 gallons or more of these substances, you will need to refer to this appendix. Shipping

85

paperwork should have "Marine Pollutant" noted, and the marine pollutant symbol must be included on the packaging.

Item Description

If shipping nonhazardous and hazardous materials simultaneously, enter a description for the hazardous material first and highlight it with a contrasting color.

Shipping Paperwork

Shipping paperwork should include the following information:

- Page numbers: if the content spans more than one page, they should indicate how many pages are included (e.g., "Page 1 of 5").
- Detailed description of each hazardous substance
- Signed shipper's certification indicating preparation in accordance with regulations

The shipper's certification should be on the original shipping paperwork unless the shipper is a private carrier. Do not accept a package that isn't safe or that clearly violates the Hazardous Materials Regulations.

The shipping paperwork will have columns labeled "HM" for hazardous material, ID#, hazard class, shipping name, and packing group. If the product being shipped is hazardous, place an "X" or "RQ" for reportable quantity in the HM column. The packing group is identified with a Roman numeral. Do not abbreviate the rest of the information, i.e., the ID#, hazard class, or shipping name.

The item description should also include the number of packages, type of packages, quantity, and unit of measure. If an item has been marked generic ("G"), then its technical name must be on the paperwork.

The shipper must add an emergency response telephone number to the shipping paperwork. This number is important for emergency responders, who will need information about how to handle the hazardous materials if there is a fire or if the materials have spilled. Emergency contacts may include the hazardous material provider or agency qualified to provide advice about how to manage hazardous materials during an emergency. The name, unique identifier, or contract number of the emergency response information (ERI) provider should be on the shipping papers.

Shippers are responsible for providing motor carriers with ERI. There should be information for each hazardous material. Carriers must be able to use the instructions a good distance away from the vehicle. It should explain how carriers should handle emergency situations, along with information about potential hazards to health, precautions that should be taken, whether there is an explosion or fire risk, and first aid measures. This information should either be on the shipping paperwork or in an emergency response guidebook.

The shipper should write the total quantity and type of the shipment before or after the item description. Units of measurement and packaging type are often abbreviated. "Waste" should also be written before the hazardous substances' shipping name. For example:

UN2191, Waste petroleum, 4, PG I

Note that nonhazardous materials do not require an identification number or hazard class on their shipping papers.

Shippers keep copies of shipping paperwork for two to three years. They will keep them for three years if hazardous waste was shipped. However, if there is only a carrier involved and not a shipper, the carrier will keep this paperwork for one year.

Learn more about regulations for transporting hazardous waste in 49 CFR 171-185.

Shipper's Certification

Shippers certify that hazardous materials are prepared according to regulations. This certification will be on the original shipping documents and will contain the signature of the shipper. An exception to this is when a private shipper is transporting its own products. Only accept packages that comply with hazardous materials regulations and don't show signs of damage. Check with carriers for additional information about handling hazardous substances. Your employer may also have transportation rules for you to follow.

Package Labels and Markings

All package labels or tags should have markings applied by shippers. When checking for markings, make sure that the name of the hazardous material indicated by the marking is the same as the one on the shipping papers. All packages should have shipping labels, names and addresses of shippers or cosigners, and the identification number and name of the material being shipped.

Look for other information on packages, such as "Marine Pollutant." Some packages include markings that indicate the direction the shipment should be sitting in, such as arrows indicating the upright position. One or more labels applied to the shipment should indicate the hazard class for each substance being transported.

Recognizing Hazardous Materials

Shipping paperwork should indicate whether a product is hazardous or not. The hazard class, identification number, and hazardous material markings should all be on the paperwork. If you do not see this information, consider the type of business the shipper is in, look for hazard placards, and look at the type of package the shipment is in. If it's in drums or cylinders, it is likely a hazardous material. If the shipping paper contains handling precautions, this could also indicate that the shipment is hazardous.

Hazard Waste Manifest

A Uniform Hazardous Waste Manifest must be signed if you transport hazardous waste. Shippers prepare, sign, and date this document. Their EPA registration number must be on it, along with those of the carrier and the destination. Waste can only be given to a recognized disposal facility. The recipient must also sign this form. Keep a copy of it for your records.

Placards and Placard Tables

Only during an emergency can you drive an improperly placarded vehicle. Otherwise, ensure that your CMV has the right placards attached. Placards should be on the front, back, and sides of the vehicle, easily viewable to other drivers. People should be able to read the placards from left to right, and all letters and numbers should be level.

Keep placards three inches away from other markings or attachments, like ladders. The background behind placards should be a contrasting color, making them easier to see. Place the front placard on the trailer or tractor of the CMV. Lastly, ensure that the right hazard class of the materials being shipped are on all placards.

Hazardous Materials

To determine which placards apply, you must know the hazard class, quantity, and weight of the hazardous materials.

The following tables contain materials that must be placarded.

Placard Table 1: Any Amount	
If vehicle contains any amount of the following:	Placard as:
1.1 Mass explosives	Explosives 1.1
1.2 Project hazards	Explosives 1.2
1.3 Mass fire hazards	Explosives 1.3
2.3 Poisonous/toxic gases	Poison gas
4.3 Dangerous when wet	Dangerous when wet
5.2 Organic peroxide, type B, liquid or solid, temperature controlled	Organic peroxide
6.1 Inhalation hazard zone A&B only	Poison/toxic inhalation
7 Radioactive yellow III label only	Radioactive

Placard Table 2: 1,001 lbs. or More	
Hazard class or division	Placard name
1.4 Minor explosion	Explosives 1.4
1.5 Very insensitive	Explosives 1.5
1.6 Extremely insensitive	Explosives 1.6
2.1 Flammable gases	Flammable gas
2.2 Nonflammable gases	Nonflammable gas
3 Flammable liquids	Flammable
Combustible liquid	Combustible**
4.1 Flammable solids	Flammable solid
4.2 Spontaneously combustible	Spontaneously combustible
5.1 Oxidizers	Oxidizer

Hazardous Materials

5.2 Other than organic peroxide, type B, liquid or solid, temperature controlled	Organic peroxide
6.1 Other than inhalation hazard zone A or B	Poison
6.2 Infectious Substances	N/A
8 Corrosives	Corrosive
9 Misc. hazardous materials	Class 9*
ORM-D	N/A
* Class 9 placard not required for domestic transportation.	
** Flammable can be used in place of combustible on cargo tank or portable tank.	

Use placards labeled "dangerous" when transporting 1,001 pounds or more of materials listed in Table 2 or when you haven't loaded 2,205 pounds of more of any of these materials in one location. However, if these items pose an inhalation hazard, "POISON GAS" or "POISON INHALATION" must be included on the packaging regardless of weight.

Display a "DANGEROUS WHEN WET" placard on items with a secondary hazard classification of "dangerous when wet." The weight limit does not apply to these items either.

On the lower corner of every placard used to distinguish primary or subsidiary hazard classes should be the hazard class or division number. If a subsidiary hazard placard does not have the class number, it can still be transported if color specifications are met.

Bulk packages with hazardous materials should always be properly placarded. Placement of those placards depends on the shipment.

Loading and Unloading

Be very careful when loading and unloading hazardous substances. Take extra care with the containers, ensuring that you do not use anything that could cause punctures or other damage to them.

Basic Rules

When you are ready to load or unload hazardous products, use the parking brake so your CMV will not move while you work. Check containers for damage. If you find a leak, report it and do not transport the package. Legally, you cannot move a CMV that has a leaking hazardous substance.

Brace containers so that they do not move during transportation. If any of the containers have valves, make sure other shipments do not push against those valves. Secure all packages as tightly as you can without causing damage. Never open packages en route to their destination. When unloading, empty packages one at a time.

Do not expose hazardous materials to heat sources. Cargo heaters are usually prohibited. Never load explosives, flammables gases, or flammable liquids into a heated cargo space. Also, do not smoke when loading or unloading hazardous materials of any kind, especially explosives, flammables, and oxidizers.

Hazardous Materials

Explosives, flammable solids, and oxidizers should be transported in a closed cargo space. They should never hang off the back of a truck unless they are water and fire resistant and are covered in resistant tarps.

Specific Precautions

Class 1: Explosives

Transporting explosives is extremely risky for your health and safety. There are specific requirements for transporting, loading, and unloading them.

To load or unload explosives, you must do the following:

- Turn off your engine
- Eliminate fuel from heat tanks and turn off heat power sources
- Remove items that could puncture the explosives, like hooks, nails, etc.
- Apply a nonferrous, Division 1.1, 1.2, or 1.3 liner to the floor of your truck

Be cautious when handling explosives. Do not throw or drop them. Do not roll them unless they are contained in kegs or barrels. They must be transported in a closed cargo transport unit. Never transfer them from one CMV to another when you are on a highway, unless there is an emergency. If you must transfer explosives, warn passersby with warning reflectors, cones, or flags.

If packages of explosives are damaged, do not transport them. Do not accept packages that are damp or have oily stains on them either.

If Division 1.1 or 1.2 explosives are part of a placarded or marked cargo tank, do not transport them in vehicle combinations. Especially if the other materials being transported are poison gas, poison, or radioactive materials labeled with "yellow III."

Class 4 and Class 5: Flammable Solids and Oxidizers

Flammable solids (class 4) can explode if exposed to heat, air, or water. They are also known to spontaneously react.

Transport class 4 and 5 materials in a completely enclosed or covered package with adequate ventilation. Keep them dry during loading and unloading to avoid reaction.

Class 8: Corrosives

Breakable containers of corrosives should be loaded and unloaded one at a time, right side up. Do not roll or drop these materials no matter what type of containers they are in. They must be loaded onto an even, flat surface.

Carboys are glass or plastic containers that can hold up to 60 liters. They're frequently used to transport corrosive liquids. Never stack them unless they can bear the weight of each other. If you're loading nitric acid, never stack it above other hazardous materials.

Corrosives should never be loaded near the following:

- Division 1.1, 1.2, or 1.3 liquids
- Division 1.4 explosives
- Division 4.1 flammable solids
- Division 1.5 blasting agents
- Division 2.3, Zone A or B poisonous gases
- Division 4.2 spontaneously combustible materials

Hazardous Materials

- Division 6.1 poison liquids
- Class 5 oxidizers

Class 2: Compressed Gases and Cryogenic Liquids

Cylinders of compressed gases and cryogenic liquids must be stored upright if racks are not available. Cylinders must be loaded horizontally so their relief valves are in vapor spaces.

Division 2.3 and 6.1: Poison Gas and Poisonous Materials

Poisonous gases and materials cannot be transported in interconnected containers. They also can't be carried in a driver's cab or near any goods meant for consumption by animals or people. To load and unload these materials, you must undergo specialized training.

Class 7: Radioactive Materials

Shippers label some radioactive materials Radioactive II or III based on the transport index. They must print the index out on the shipping label for reference. Because radiation passes through packages, it can only be loaded with a certain number of other packages. There are regulations for how close any person or animal can be to these materials.

The transport index describes how to handle these substances during transportation. The transport index of materials transported should never exceed 50. Table A in the 49 CFR 177-842 contains rules for the transport index. Proximity limitations are provided by this index.

Total Transport Index	Minimum separation distance in meters (feet) to nearest undeveloped film in various times of transit					Min. distance in meters (feet) to people or diving partition of cargo depts.
	Up to 2 hours	2-4 hours	4-8 hours	8-12 hours	Over 12 hours	
None	0.0 (0)	0.0 (0)	0.0 (0)	0.0 (0)	0.0 (0)	0.0 (0)
0.1 to 1.0	0.3 (1)	0.6 (2)	0.9 (3)	1.2 (4)	1.5 (5)	0.3 (1)
1.1 to 5.0	0.9 (3)	1.2 (4)	1.8 (6)	2.4 (8)	3.4 (11)	0.6 (2)
5.1 to 10.0	1.2 (4)	1.8 (6)	2.7 (9)	3.4 (11)	4.6 (15)	0.9 (3)
10.1 to 20.0	1.5 (5)	2.4 (8)	3.7 (12)	4.9 (16)	6.7 (22)	1.2 (4)
20.1 to 30.0	2.1 (7)	3.0 (10)	4.6 (15)	6.1 (20)	8.8 (29)	1.5 (5)
30.1 to 40.0	2.4 (8)	3.4 (11)	5.2 (17)	6.7 (22)	10.1 (33)	1.8 (6)
40.1 to 50.0	2.7 (9)	3.7 (12)	5.8 (19)	7.3 (24)	11.0 (36)	2.1 (7)

Hazardous Materials

Mixed Loads

Some hazardous materials must be loaded separately and in different cargo spaces. The following table indicates these substances.

Segregation Table for Hazardous Materials/Do Not Load Table	
Do not load:	**In same vehicle with:**
Division 6.1 or 2.3 poison or poison inhalation hazard material	Human or animal food unless poison package is over-packed in an approved way. Foodstuffs are anything you swallow. Mouthwash, toothpaste, and skin creams aren't foodstuff.
Division 2.3 poisonous gas Zone A or Division 6.1 poison liquids, PGI, Zone A	Division 1.1, 1.2, 1.3 Explosives, Division 5.1 (Oxidizers), Class 3 (Flammable Liquids), Class 8 (Corrosive Liquids), Division 5.2 (Organic Peroxides), Division 1.1, 1.2, 1.3 Explosives, Division 1.5 (Blasting Agents), Division2.1 (Flammable Gases), Class 4 (Flammable Solids)
Charge stored batteries	Division 1.1
Class 1 detonating primers	Any other explosives unless in authorized containers or packages
Division 6.1 detonating primers	Any other explosives unless in authorized containers or packages
Division 6.1 cyanides or cyanide mixtures	Acids, corrosive materials, or other acidic materials which could release hydrocyanic acid (e.g., Cyanides, Inorganic, n.o.s. Silver Cyanide Sodium Cyanide)
Class 8 nitric acid	Other materials unless the nitric acid is not loaded above any other material

Bulk Packaging Marking, Loading, and Unloading

"Bulk" refers to packages that are over 882 or have a volume of 119 gallons. There are two primary types of bulk packages: cargo tanks and portable tanks. Portable tanks can be removed from the vehicle transporting them while cargo tanks cannot.

Markings

ID numbers of hazardous materials must be clearly displayed on bulk packaging. For a complete list of these numbers, refer to the Hazardous Materials Table. Regulation Section 172.332(a) requires ID numbers to be displayed on placards, white square-on-point configurations, or orange panels. Ensure that re-test dates are shown on specification cargo tanks. A specification cargo tank is one that had to be welded onto a CMV.

Hazardous Materials

Content shipping names and the names of the owner or lessees need to be displayed on opposite sides of portable tanks. If a portable tank has less than 1,000 gallons, then the shipping name letters should be one-inch tall, and the ID number should be posted on opposite sides of the tank. If the capacity is more than 1,000 gallons, then the letters need to be two-inches tall, and the ID number needs to be posted on all sides and ends of the tank.

Tank Loading

All tank loading and unloaded must be monitored by a qualified supervisor. The supervisor should be alert and stand within 25 feet of the tank being loaded or unloaded. They need to be able to see the delivery hose and tank clearly. This person should be informed which hazardous materials are being handled so that they can act in case of an emergency. They may need to move the cargo tank, so it's imperative that they are qualified. Before moving tanks that contain hazardous substances, close all valves and manholes to prevent leaks.

Flammable Liquids

If handling flammable liquids, make sure your engine is turned off unless you need to use a pump. If you must fill a cargo tank from an open filling hole, make sure that the tank is grounded securely before and during the process.

Compressed Gas

Unless you're loading and unloading, liquid discharge valves should remain closed. As with flammable liquids, only keep the engine on when a pump is being used. Turn the engine off before you unhook the hose used. If you're transferring a chlorine cargo tank, everything must be unhooked before uncoupling or coupling. Use wheel chocks to keep trailers from moving when you uncouple from power units. Wheel chocks are blocks or wedges placed in front of or behind wheels to keep a vehicle from rolling.

Driving and Parking Rules

Parking with Division 1.1, 1.2, or 1.3 Explosives

Do not park within 5 feet of the traveled part of the highway when carrying these explosives. Unless absolutely necessary, you shouldn't park within 300 feet of the following structures:

- Bridge
- Tunnel
- Building
- Gathering place
- An open fire
- Private property
- Shipper's property
- Carrier's property
- Consignee's property

You can only leave your CMV unattended in an approved place, like a safe haven. Local authorities typically decide what constitutes a safe haven.

Parking a Placarded Vehicle Not Transporting Division 1.1, 1.2, or 1.3 Explosives

It's acceptable to briefly park a placarded vehicle that isn't weighed down with explosives within 5 feet of the traveled part of a road if it's required by your job. The vehicle must be monitored while it is parked

93

Hazardous Materials

there. Don't leave a trailer full of hazardous materials on or near a public street. You should also never park within 300 feet of an open fire.

Attended Parked Vehicles

If you're monitoring a parked vehicle, stay awake and alert. Do not get in the sleeper berth. You must remain in the vehicle. If you must get out, remain within 100 feet so it stays within your sight. Be mindful that you are transporting hazardous materials. Learn what you need to do in case of an emergency. If you need to move the vehicle, then first make sure it is safe to do so.

No Flares!

If your CMV breaks down, you will need to use stopped vehicle signals. Burn signals, like fuses and flares, cannot be used if you're carrying a tank made for flammable materials, regardless of whether it is full or empty. You also can't use them if you're carrying Division 1.1, 1.2, or 1.3 explosives. The best signals to use are red electric lights or reflective triangles.

Route Restrictions

Be aware that you may need a permit to transport hazardous waste or materials through certain counties and/or states. The number of routes you can take may be limited. Local rules for transporting hazardous materials are frequently updated, so find out what you need before traveling through certain locations. All shipping paperwork needs to be in order.

A dispatcher can tell you about required permits and route restrictions if you work for a carrier. You will need to consult state agencies for this information if you are an independent trucker. There may be additional restrictions if you are transporting hazardous goods over bridges or through tunnels.

If your vehicle is placarded, do not drive through heavily populated areas, alleys, tunnels, or narrow streets unless there is no alternative. Do your best to find alternate routes.

Do not drive near open fires. Ask the carrier for a written route plan for the transportation of Division 1.1, 1.2, or 1.3 explosives. If you need to plan the routes yourself, plan ahead and always keep a copy of those routes on paper. Dangerous shipments can only be delivered to authorized individuals or designated, locked explosives storage facilities.

The carrier plans the best routes for placarded radioactive material transportation. Obtain these plans from them when you pick up your shipment.

No Smoking

If transporting Division 2.1 gases or Class 3 flammable liquids in a placarded cargo tank, do not smoke within 25 feet of them. Do not carry lit pipes, cigars, or cigarettes within 25 feet of them either. You also cannot carry these lit items or smoke within 25 feet of:

- Class 1 explosives
- Class 3 flammable liquids
- Class 4.1 flammable solids
- Class 4.2 spontaneously combustible products
- Class 5 oxidizers

Hazardous Materials

Refuel with Engine Off
Don't fuel up a CMV carrying hazardous materials until your engine is turned off. Do not leave the gas nozzle unattended.

10 BC Fire Extinguisher
Placarded vehicles must have a 10 BC rated fire extinguisher on the power unit.

Check Tires
Your CMV's tires should always be properly inflated. Check your tires at the start of a road trip and whenever you park with a tire pressure gauge. If you find a leaking or flat tire, find somewhere safe to fix it. Do not ignore it and continue with your trip. Overheated tires must be removed and placed a safe distance away from your CMV. Do not get back on the road until the issue has been resolved. Parking and attending rules for placarded vehicles apply in these situations.

Where to Keep Shipping Papers and Emergency Response Information
If the shipment paperwork has any discrepancies, do not accept it. This paperwork must be easy to find in the event of an accident. Keep the hazardous materials shipping paperwork separate from all other paperwork. Keep the paperwork in a place where you can easily grab it. This could be on the driver's side door in a pouch. When you leave the vehicle, leave the papers behind either in the driver's seat or in that pouch.

Papers for Division 1.1, 1.2, or 1.3 Explosives
The carrier for these explosives should give you a copy of the Federal Carrier Safety Regulations (FMCSR), Part 397. They should also provide you with instructions on how to handle an emergency. The following information should be in those instructions:

- Contact info for the carrier agents or shippers
- Description of explosives
- Emergency precautions in case of fires, leaks, or other accidents

There should be a receipt for these documents, which you are required to sign. While driving, you should always have:

- A copy of FMCSR, Part 397
- Written route plan
- Emergency instructions
- Shipping papers

Equipment for Chlorine
An approved gas mask is required if you are transporting chlorine. Have an emergency kit ready in case there are leaks in the cargo tank's dome cover plate fittings.

Stop Before Railroad Crossings
If you're driving a placarded vehicle, carrying chlorine, or transporting cargo tanks for hazardous materials, stop before a railroad crossing. Stop within 15 to 50 feet from the rail. Wait until it's clear that no train is coming before you cross. Never shift gears when you are crossing.

Emergencies

Emergency Response Guidebook (ERG)

The ERG is a guidebook from the Department of Transportation for industry workers, police, and firefighters. It explains how they should protect the public and themselves from hazardous substances. Information is organized by shipping name and hazardous material ID numbers. This information should also be on the shipping papers, which emergency personnel will reference during an emergency.

Crashes/Incidents

In the event of an accident, do the following:

- If you have a driving partner, make sure they're ok.
- Grab the shipping papers and keep them on you.
- Tell people to stand upwind from the scene and as far away as possible.
- Warn people of the danger.
- Call for help.

If an accident happens, make sure that the scene is clear of bystanders. If there is a spill, try to limit the spread of the hazardous material if possible. When emergency personnel arrive, tell them how dangerous the material is and hand them the shipping paperwork and emergency response documents.

Fires

Only specially trained individuals in protective gear can control hazardous material fires. Do not attempt to do it if you don't have the training. If there's a fire, call for help. If the fire is small, a fire extinguisher might help, but firefighters still need to come to the scene.

Do not open a trailer door if it feels hot because the cargo may be on fire. If the cargo is aflame, don't try to fight it yourself. When emergency personnel arrive, hand them the emergency response and shipping paperwork. Warn bystanders and passersby of the danger so that they will maintain their distance.

If there is a cargo leak, try to identify the material via the package location, labels, or shipping paperwork. Don't touch the leaked material; it could seriously injure you. Trying to identify a material by smell is ineffective. Toxic gases often ruin people's sense of smell. Inhaling odorless gases can be harmful or even fatal.

If there is a hazardous materials leak, do not smoke, eat, or drink around it. Once you recognize that there's a leak, don't try to move the vehicle further except to get off the road and away from crowded places. If you can move the CMV without endangering others, do so if there is no alternative.

Once you discover a hazardous substance leak, stop driving, park the vehicle, and secure the area. Do not leave the scene. If you cannot call for help, ask someone else nearby to do it. Make sure that person has all the information they need to describe the accident, including your name, the carrier's information, the location of the emergency, and direction of travel. They also need to know the shipping name and hazard class ID. Write this information down so they don't have to remember it.

Moving a vehicle that has a hazardous material leak could cause contamination, so don't do it unless it is necessary. Do not try to salvage spilled goods by repacking the containers. Only trained professionals can repair hazardous material leaks.

Responses to Specific Hazards

Class 1 Explosives
If you break down or have an accident while carrying explosive materials, warn bystanders. Tell people not to smoke near the accident. A fire could result in explosion, so make sure that everyone around is aware.

If there is a collision while carrying explosives, you will need to move the explosives 200 feet from the vehicles and occupied spaces. Call your supervisor for instructions if you aren't sure how to remove the explosives safely. Maintain a safe distance from the scene after you have removed the explosives.

Class 2 Compressed Gases
Immediately warn people if compressed gas leaks from your CMV. Only personnel trained to handle the leak can go near it. Call the shipper and let them know there's been an accident.

Do not transfer flammable compressed gas between tanks on a public road unless you're fueling machinery.

Class 3 Flammable Liquids
If you have an emergency while transporting flammable liquids, warn people to keep away. Tell them not to smoke anywhere near the vehicle.

If a cargo tank is leaking flammable liquids, get off the road as quickly as you can. Don't transfer the products between vehicles on public roads unless it becomes necessary to do so.

Class 4 Flammable Solids and Class 5 Oxidizing Materials
Spilling these types of materials poses a fire risk, so warn everyone present. If packages of the Class 4 products are smoldering, do not open them. Only move them from your CMV if you can do it safely. If it will decrease the fire risk, remove all unbroken packages.

Class 6 Poisonous Materials and Infectious Substances
Protect yourself, others, and your property from harm as best as you can when an incident arises with these substances. Some poisonous substances are also flammable, so you would use the same precautions as you would for Class 4 and 5 materials. Keep away from open flames and don't allow anyone to smoke near the substances.

If your CMV experienced a poison or poisonous gas leak, it must be inspected for remnants of the poison before you can drive it again.

Contact your supervisor if the infectious substances you're transporting are damaged. Don't accept any packages that have leaks or appear to be damaged.

Class 7 Radioactive Materials
Report leaks and broken packages of these substances to your supervisor or dispatcher. Do not inhale the material and do not touch it. You won't be able to drive the vehicle again until it has passed inspection for traces of the material and has been cleaned.

Class 8 Corrosive Materials
If corrosives spill in your vehicle, it will have to be thoroughly rinsed out with water before reloading. Transporting a leaking tank of corrosives could be dangerous, so pull off the road if you feel unsafe. There may be fumes, so keep bystanders away from them. If you can contain the liquid that is leaking, do so. But if you can't, call your supervisor or dispatcher for guidance.

Required Notification

Police and firefighters refer to the National Response Center when there is an incident involving chemical hazards. It has a 24-hour, toll-free line. You or your employer need to call if any of the following events happen:

- Someone is killed
- Someone is injured and needs to be hospitalized
- The general public had to evacuate for more than one hour
- A major transportation facility had to close for more than one hour
- Suspected radioactive contamination, fire, breakage, or spill have occurred
- There's been a spill or other accident involving infections substances
- More than 119 gallons of liquid or 882 pounds of solid marine pollutant spilled

The number for the National Response Center is **(800) 424-8802**. When calling, be prepared to provide the following information:

- Your name
- Name and address of the carrier
- Date, time, and location of the incident
- If there are injuries, what type
- Name, quantity, and classification of hazardous materials involved
- Nature of the accident involving hazardous materials and if the scene is still dangerous
- If accident involves reportable quantity, include shipper name and quantity of hazardous substance

Your employer will need this information. The shipment's carrier is required to follow up with a written report up to 30 days after the incident.

You can also contact the Chemical Transportation Emergency Center (CHEMTREC). Their number is **(800) 424-9300**, and it's available toll-free for 24 hours. CHEMTREC provides emergency personnel with information about hazardous materials' physical properties. It communicates with the National Response Center, so no matter which one you call, it will inform the other.

Hazardous Materials

Radioactive Separation Table A

The following table explains how long you can leave radioactive yellow – II or yellow – III packages near film, people, or animals.

Transport Total Index	Min. Distance in Feet to Nearest Undeveloped Film					To People or Cargo Compartment Partitions
	0-2 hours	2-4 hours	4-8 hours	8-12 hours	Over 12 hours	
None	0	0	0	0	0	0
0.1-1.0	1	2	3	4	5	1
1.1-5.0	3	4	6	8	11	2
5.1-10.0	4	6	9	11	15	3
10.1-20.0	5	8	12	16	22	4
20.1-30.0	7	10	15	20	29	5
30.1-40.0	8	11	17	22	33	6
40.1-50.0	9	12	19	24	36	N/A

Hazard Class Definitions Table B

The following table is pretty much the hazardous materials table revamped. It identifies the classes of hazardous materials in the nine major categories and shows additional ones for combustible liquids and consumer commodities.

Class	Class Name	Example
1	Explosives	Ammunition, Dynamite, Fireworks
2	Gases	Propane, Oxygen, Helium
3	Flammable	Gasoline, Acetone
4	Flammable Solids	Matches, Fuses
5	Oxidizers	Ammonium Nitrate, Hydrogen Peroxide
6	Poisons	Pesticides, Arsenic
7	Radioactive	Uranium, Plutonium
8	Corrosives	Hydrochloric Acid, Battery Fluid
9	Miscellaneous Hazardous Materials	Formaldehyde, Asbestos
None	ORM-D (Other Regulated Material-Domestic)	Hair Spray or Charcoal
None	Combustible Liquids	Fuel Oils, Lighter Fluid

Hazardous Materials Glossary

This glossary defines terms that were used in this guide along with others you may encounter as a CMV driver. For the full glossary, refer to the Hazardous Materials Rules, 49 CFR 171.8. While you don't need to memorize these terms, it's a good idea to obtain a copy of the most recent version of the Hazardous Materials Rules.

Bulk Packaging: Packages other than vessels or barges, like freight containers or transport vehicles, used to contain hazardous materials with no intermediate form of containment. Meets the following requirements:

1. A maximum capacity greater than 450 L (119 gallons) as a receptacle for a liquid

2. A maximum net mass greater than 400 kg (882 pounds) and a maximum capacity greater than 450 L (119 gallons) as a receptacle for a solid

3. A water capacity greater than 454 kg (1000 pounds) as a receptacle for a gas as defined in Sec. 173.115

Hazardous Materials

Cargo tank: A type of bulk packaging, which is:

1. A tank primarily used to carry liquids or gases and includes appurtenances, reinforcements, fittings, and closures (for "tank," see 49 CFR 178.345-1(c), 178.337-1, or 178.338-1, as applicable)

2. is temporarily part of a motor vehicle that, by reason of its size, construction, or attachment to a motor vehicle, is loaded or unloaded without being removed from it

3. isn't fabricated under a specification for tank cars, portable tanks, cylinders, etc.

Carrier: An individual participating in the transportation of passengers or property on either land, water, contract, private carrier, or by civil aircraft.

Consignee: The destined recipient of the shipment.

Division: Part of a hazard class

EPA: U.S. Environmental Protection Agency

FMCSR: Federal Motor Carrier Safety Regulations

Freight Container: A container that has a volume of 64 cubic feet or more, which is designed and constructed to allow it to be lifted with its contents intact, intended mainly to contain packages during transportation.

Fuel Tank: A transport tank used to ship flammable or combustible liquids or compressed gas to provide fuel for the vehicle to which it is attached.

Gross Weight or Gross Mass: The weight of a package and its contents.

Hazard Class: The defining criteria for hazard classes listed in Part 173 and the 172.i01 table. Materials will only be assigned one hazard class, even if they fit the criteria for more than one.

Hazardous Materials: As determined by the Secretary of Transportation, an item or substance that may pose an unreasonable risk to safety, health, and property when transported. Items are further defined under Sec. 172.101 and 172.102, and they meet criteria for hazard classes in part 173. Hazardous materials include mixtures and solutions in Appendix A to Sec. 172.101 and equals or exceeds reportable quantities.

Hazardous Waste: According to 40 CFR Part 262, a hazardous waste manifest is any material subject to the hazardous waste manifest requirements of the U.S. Environmental Protection Agency.

Limited quantity: The maximum amount of a hazardous material, which must have special labeling or packaging.

Marking: The ID number, instructions, specifications, name, precautions, and UN marks that go on the outside of a hazardous material's packaging.

Mixture: A product that's made of two or more chemical compounds or elements.

Name of contents: As recommended in Sec. 172.101, the correct name of a shipment.

P.S.I. or psi: Pounds per square inch.

101

P.S.I.A. or psia: Pounds per square inch absolute.

Reportable Quantity (RQ): For materials identified in Column 1 of Appendix A, the amount specified in the third column of the Appendix to Sec. 172.101.

PHMSA: Pipeline and Hazardous Materials Safety Administration

Shipper's Certification: Legal statement on shipping paperwork that says shipper prepared package according to regulations, which is signed by the shipper.

Statements may be one of the following:

"This is to certify that the above-named materials are properly classified, described, packaged, marked and labeled, and are in proper condition for transportation according to the applicable regulations of the Department of Transportation."

"I hereby declare that the contents of this consignment are fully and accurately described above the proper shipping name and are classified, packed, marked and labeled, and are in all respects in proper condition for transport according to applicable international and national government regulations."

The exact wording can be modified to include the type of transportation used.

Shipping Paper: Document that accompanies the shipment that must include information specified in Sec. 172.202, 172.203, and 172.204.

Technical Name: The proper name of a chemical as used in technical handbooks or scientific texts.

Transport Vehicle: A vehicle like a tractor trailer, truck, tank car, or rail car that carries cargo.

UN: United Nations

UN Standard Packaging: Special packaging the meets the requirements defined in in Subpart L and M of Part 178.

Practice Quiz

1. Which of the following is a hazardous material?
    a. Cardboard
    b. Plastic packaging
    c. Laundry detergent
    d. Aerosol cans

2. Which part of the 49 Code of Federal Regulations (CFR) contains information about hazardous materials?
    a. Part 171
    b. Part 40
    c. Part 655
    d. Part 50

3. Which of the following people initially makes sure that products being shipped are labeled properly with ID numbers and warning labels?
    a. Driver
    b. Manufacturer
    c. Carrier
    d. Shipper

4. Under which of the following conditions should a transporter reject a shipment?
    a. The labeling is legible.
    b. The packaging is leaking.
    c. The shipment is in clear packaging.
    d. The warning labels used are too bright.

5. Hazardous materials are classified under nine _____.
    a. Color categories
    b. Weight limits
    c. Hazard classes
    d. Package regulations

Answer Explanations

1. C: Laundry detergent is a hazardous material. Choices *A*, *B*, and *D* are incorrect because they are not hazardous materials.

2. A: Choice *A* is correct because part 171 contains information about hazardous materials. Choice *B* is incorrect because part 40 refers to workplace drug and alcohol testing. Choice *C* is incorrect because part 655 refers to alcohol and drug use in transit operations. Choice *D* is incorrect because part 50 refers to national primary and secondary ambient air quality standards.

3. D: Choice *D* is correct because the shipper initially ensures that products being shipped are labeled properly and have ID numbers and warning labels. Choices *A*, *B*, and *C* are incorrect; while these people have the responsibility to check the product information to some degree, the shipper is the first person to ensure that labels, ID numbers, etc. are added to the packages.

4. B: The transporter should never accept a shipment that is leaking. Choice *A* is incorrect; a label that's easy to read is ideal. Choice *C* is incorrect because clear packaging does not make a shipment unsafe to transport. Choice *D* is incorrect; the brightness of the warning label has no effect on the transport of the shipment.

5. C: Hazardous materials are classified under nine hazard classes. The remaining choices are incorrect because hazardous materials are not classified under color categories, weight limits, or package regulations.

School Buses

Danger Zones and Use of Mirrors

School bus drivers take considerable safety precautions to ensure the safety of schoolchildren. Vigilant bus drivers pay close attention to danger zones. Danger zones are places around the bus where children face the highest risk of accident or injury.

Bus drivers mitigate some of the dangers for their passengers by properly using all mirrors. Of course, bus drivers cannot see around every side of their buses, nor can they see every inch behind their buses. The use of mirrors helps bus drivers see anyone who might be in a danger zone. Danger zones extend twelve feet from both sides of the bus, as well as twelve feet from the rear. In front of the bus, the danger zone includes an area of up to thirty feet; the first twelve feet from the front of the bus are the most dangerous part of the front danger zone. A school bus driver's ability to see is compromised when children stand within twelve feet of both sides of the bus, as well as within twelve feet from the front or back of the bus. The left side of the bus presents an additional risk from oncoming traffic.

Given the risks, school bus drivers must set their mirrors before driving. School bus drivers use the outside flat mirrors—located on the right and left sides of the windshield—to navigate traffic safely. Bus drivers use these mirrors to spot traffic on either side of the bus, to look before safely merging into traffic, to check for obstacles on roads and in parking lots, and to keep an eye on pedestrians on either side of their buses. Bus drivers must be aware of three blind spots: underneath these mirrors, behind them, and from the back bumper of the bus to a distance of up to 400 feet. Bus drivers should be able to see a distance equivalent to four times the length of a single bus, to the rear, with their flat mirrors. The outside flat mirrors are positioned correctly when they see down both sides of the bus, the bus tires, and the ground.

Mirror Types

The outside left and right convex mirrors work in tandem with the outside left and right flat mirrors. Use these mirrors to obtain a wide view of objects on either side of the bus. While the convex mirrors spot objects that the flat mirrors miss, these mirrors present a distorted view of objects. Note that the size of objects detected by these mirrors is inaccurate. The location of these objects in relation to the bus is also inaccurate. Properly adjust these mirrors to ensure that they detect both the sides of the bus, the front tires, and a traffic lane.

Crossover mirrors provide more visibility to blind spots in front of the bus. The crossover mirrors on both sides provide a sweeping view across the hood of the bus. Correctly set these mirrors by ensuring that there is no gap between the two regions in front of the bus that the crossover mirrors cover. Used together, the flat mirrors, convex mirrors, and crossover mirrors provide a panoramic view of the sides, front, and back of the bus.

Finally, use the overhead inside rearview mirror to ensure the safety of passengers inside the bus. While transporting children to and from school, you are in charge of the children, so you must ensure that student behavior conforms to school policy about appropriate school bus safety procedures. Adjust the overhead inside rearview mirror to see every row of seats on the bus, as well as the highest point of the rear window at the back of the bus. Make sure to use all mirrors to ensure the safety of children, in danger zones and elsewhere.

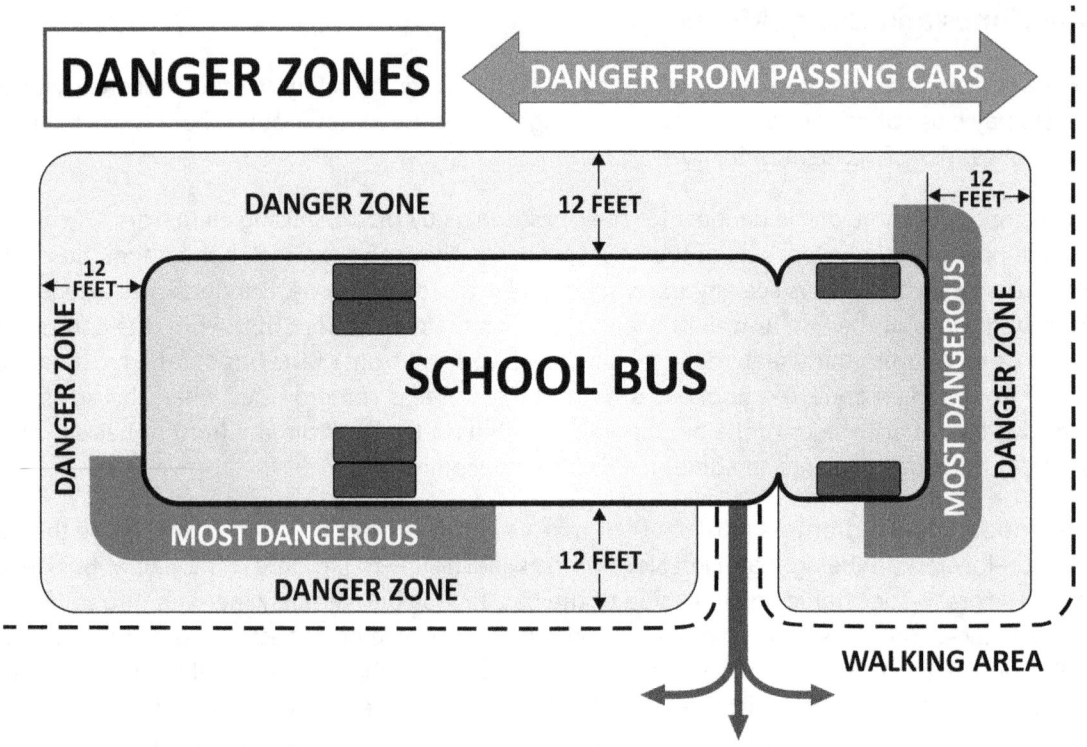

Loading and Unloading

Passengers face a greater risk of injury or death outside of the school bus than they do inside of it. On average, more fatalities among schoolchildren occur during loading and unloading procedures than occur because of motor-vehicle accidents. School bus drivers must comprehend the risks schoolchildren face, memorize general loading and unloading procedures—as well as specific state and local loading and unloading procedures—and proper protocol. Proper loading and unloading procedures mitigate the risks to schoolchildren.

Much foresight goes into the planning of school bus routes. Each bus route follows an established course of designated bus stops. Bus route planners establish safe bus stops by evaluating a variety of factors that impact the safety of schoolchildren, so school bus drivers must stop only at these predetermined stops. This rule applies both to picking up and dropping off. Predetermined bus stops relieve uncertainty on the part of bus drivers and children, which decreases the likelihood that human error will lead to injury or death. Only written documents can verify amendments to existing bus routes.

At the Bus Stop
When near bus stops, practice extreme vigilance and follow general and specific state and local rules. Drive slowly near bus stops and use the mirrors to scan for anyone or anything that may affect the safe loading and unloading. Use the bright loading and unloading lights within 200 feet of each bus stop and use the turn signal at least 100 feet prior to each bus stop. These procedures clearly communicate to other drivers and pedestrians the intent to begin the loading or unloading process. Before beginning to load or unload, tightly position the bus on the right side of the road where children enter and exit the bus.

Passengers walk across the bus's front, side, or rear danger zones when loading or unloading. Therefore, when stopping at a bus stop, you must leave room between the bus and any passengers waiting to be loaded onto the bus. Leave a minimum of 10 feet between the front of the bus and where the waiting passengers stand.

Depending on the bus's transmission, put the bus in either park or neutral when loading or unloading passengers. If the bus is in neutral, the parking brake must be used as well. Ensure that surrounding traffic is appropriately conforming to traffic laws before opening the door and allowing children to begin the loading or unloading process.

Approaching the Bus

After carefully stopping at the bus stop, begin the loading process, working collaboratively with the children to ensure safety. Schoolchildren should look at the bus as it approaches and stand at their designated stop. They should not fool around at the bus stop or have their backs turned toward the bus. It is your responsibility to correct unsafe behavior as warranted.

Before children approach the bus, they should confirm that you have signaled them to approach. Non-verbal communication breakdowns between bus drivers and children may result in accidents. After signaling for children to approach the bus, use your mirrors to observe the road and surrounding area for threats.

Driver Rapport and Student Behavior

Having good rapport with the children who ride your bus goes a long way to ensure safe loading and unloading. You do much to ensure the safety of passengers simply by learning the names of each child on your bus route. You should also know how many schoolchildren enter the bus at each stop.

Passengers should board the school bus slowly and carefully. You may prompt children to rely on physical supports, like handrails, to safely mount the steps of the bus. For better visibility of steep stairs, ensure that the overhead light is on while children board the bus.

In many cases, especially at younger ages, children rely on adults and authority figures to guide them. Be vigilant in case any students need your guidance throughout the loading or unloading processes. Make sure never to drive away from a bus stop until every student has found a seat. The school bus should move only once everyone is seated and facing the front of the bus. Use your interior mirror to assess student behavior and ensure conformity to proper loading procedures.

Leaving the Bus Stop

Before departure from a bus stop, use the exterior mirrors to determine whether any children remain outside. Perhaps one or more children are late for the bus in the morning; ensure that no one is desperately running after the bus on foot. If you cannot find one or more passengers, conduct a thorough search of the area around and under the bus.

Once you determine that the children are safely loaded, begin to move from the bus stop by first closing the door and putting on your seatbelt. Then set the transmission and release the parking brake. Next, turn off the flashing lights on the sides of the bus and turn on the left turn signal, which indicates to other drivers that you intend to rejoin the flow of traffic. Carefully complete these steps as you evaluate traffic with the exterior mirrors. After yielding to oncoming traffic, merge back onto the road.

While you must respond to local nuances and adapt appropriately to every situation, you should complete the same general loading process at every bus stop. Depending on the state where you operate, you will

have to conform to state-specific procedures when loading children on school grounds. Some states may require that you turn the engine off, remove the key, and exit the bus to observe children as they enter the bus.

Unloading on School Grounds and On Route

Unloading procedures are different on school grounds than they are en route. En route, at each stop, prompt children to stand no less than ten feet from the bus. This ensures that you can see children while they wait outside the bus. On school grounds, situate yourself inside or outside the bus—according to state regulations—to supervise the organized mass exit from the bus and prompt students to briskly clear the area immediately outside the doors of the bus. En route, ensure that the correct number of children exits the bus at each stop (take note that this number may differ from the number of children who embark at each stop in the morning). On school grounds, turn off the engine before unloading, and take the key with you if you leave your seat.

When they are unloaded en route, children must often cross roadways, and some of these roadways have high volumes of traffic. Parents, teachers, and bus drivers work together to ensure that children understand how to cross roadways safely; bus drivers must do their part to ensure that children follow safety procedures. The bus should not move until children are no less than ten feet from the side and front of the bus. If you can see the child's sneakers, that means that the child is a safe distance from the bus.

Of course, children must take measures to ensure their own safety, such as checking the road for traffic. You should provide them with a signal that indicates when it is safe to cross; signal twice: once before children leave the right side of the road, and a second time before they move into the left lane of traffic.

Despite the differences between unloading procedures on school grounds and en route, there are still many similarities. In both instances, you will need to approach the unloading zone safely while the children remain in their seats until the bus comes to a complete stop. They should only leave when you prompt them. Observe each student as they disembark; if you do not see a student clear the bus's danger zones, then you should get out of the bus and look for the student.

Dangerous Scenarios and Post-Trip Inspection

Students may drop personal items while exiting the bus. They should alert you when this happens, but they may act impulsively and try to retrieve the dropped item without first alerting you. They could also get caught on handrails or by the bus's doors. Therefore, be sure to watch every student clear the bus's danger zones before departing the unloading zone.

At the end of every trip, complete a thorough inspection of the bus. Children may hide in seats, fall asleep, or forget personal items like books, phones, and backpacks. Check the bus for damage caused either by normal wear and tear or delinquency, and complete thorough reports of any discrepancies.

Emergency Exit and Evacuation

Motor vehicles are prone to mechanical failures and accidents, so you must always be prepared for emergency situations. Designating responsible children as emergency aides is one of the best ways to plan for emergency situations. While every child on the bus should be familiar with proper evacuation procedures, responsible children may operate safety doors and identify safe meeting locations outside the bus.

Students responsible for picking safe meeting locations should identify locations greater than 99 feet from the road, where the wind will not blow smoke from fires into the eyes and lungs of the evacuated passengers. If an accident occurs on railroad tracks, student aides should lead classmates far away from the tracks, and, when toxins are present, they should identify a safe meeting location greater than 299 feet from the bus. In the event of a natural disaster, student aides should guide their classmates to locations where they will not be affected. You will need to assist student aides; they may not be aware of the extent of the emergency, if toxins or fires are present, etc., and they will rely on your direction.

While responding appropriately to emergency situations starts with preparedness, your ability to assess the emergency determines success. In many instances when time is not a factor, you should consult with dispatchers and supervisors before making an executive decision about how to respond. In addition to their knowledge of proper safety protocols, supervisors and dispatchers may have access to information about weather events and other disasters that you lack.

It is best to leave children on the bus when there is no sign or scent of gasoline or fire and when the bus is not in a direct collision course with other automobiles or natural disasters, like flash floods. By default, keep schoolchildren on the bus, but if circumstances require an evacuation, assess potential dangers and then evacuate.

Evacuation Procedures

Before evacuating, determine that conditions outside the bus would not endanger riders. Live wires and toppled infrastructure indicate a threat, as does the presence of unknown liquid chemicals or other contaminants. Additionally, be wary of moving any children who have suffered injuries, as movement may exacerbate injuries. You must evacuate when fire is present, when impact with other automobiles or objects is unavoidable, when a chemical contaminant is present, when the bus is in a transient or unsecured position, and when a bus is stuck on a highway ramp or railroad track.

You must also decide the best way to evacuate. Some emergencies prohibit the use of certain exit doors. In the event of engine fires, you may determine that the front door is unsafe to use and prompt children to exit from the side or rear doors instead. In the case of side door or rear door exits, a designated student aide may hold the door open for their classmates. In the event of flash floods and other emergencies where lateral, front, and rear exits are unavailable, you may prompt children to exit via the roof hatch.

Before any evacuation, follow the same engine procedures for unloading the bus on school property. Set the bus to park or neutral and activate the parking brake. Then, turn the buses off and take the keys with you when you exit. Lastly, turn on the hazard lights to signal the bus's location to pedestrians, emergency responders, and passing vehicles.

When time permits, communicate your whereabouts to dispatchers, along with scenario-specific information and information related to the types of supports required. Make future communication with dispatchers possible by hanging the talking device outside the driver's window. You may approach an evacuated bus to use such devices when warranted. When required, you may prompt pedestrians or, when no other options are available, responsible children to locate help.

You should be the last to leave the bus in an evacuation. You must stay behind to double-check the bus for any passengers who may be hidden or impaired and secure emergency utilities like traffic cones. Once

the students are safe in a designated safety location, outline this location with traffic cones. Wait with the children at the evacuation site until emergency personnel arrive.

Railroad-Highway Crossings

School bus drivers must understand the difference between active and passive railroad crossings and know how to interpret the different types of railroad signs and markings. Active railroad crossings feature automated signs and markings that tell drivers when to cross the tracks and when to yield to trains. They may also feature gates that descend to block the way when a train is coming. Passive railroad crossings, by contrast, have static signs that do not move or flash in response to changes in rail traffic; drivers must use their best judgement to determine when it is safe to cross.

Black and yellow traffic signs precede many railroad crossing sites and serve as your first warning. Treat these signs as you would treat a yield sign and slow down as you approach the railroad crossing site. Sometimes, road markings fulfill the same function as black and yellow traffic signs. Proceed with caution when you encounter railroad warning symbols on the road.

At some railroad crossing sites, white lines come before the railroad tracks, transversal to the roadway. You must keep the bus entirely behind these white lines when coming to a stop before a railroad track. In the absence of white traffic lines, defer to familiar railroad crossing signs, stopping before them. These signs may also indicate the presence of additional sets of tracks. Stop one time, at the start of the crossing and before all tracks. Then drive across all the tracks without stopping. You may also encounter gates, flashing lights, and bells. Bring the bus to a stop when any of these indicators are active. If these indicators remain active for an inordinately long time after the train has passed, seek guidance from your supervisor; do not disregard gates, flashing lights, or bells.

Proper Railroad Crossing Procedures

Approach railroad crossing sites the same way each time. First, decrease your speed and, when applicable, down-shift to a low gear. For safety reasons, check your brakes to ensure that they respond well. At least 200 feet before the railroad crossing, turn on your flashing caution lights. Next, survey the area, assessing traffic in the rearview mirrors. Move the bus to the far-right traffic lane to avoid accidents with oncoming traffic in the left lane. Simultaneously devise a backup plan in case circumstances force evacuation from the area.

Stop at least 15 feet away but no more than 50 feet from the railroad tracks. This distance ensures that you can monitor activity on and around the tracks. Next, put the bus in park or neutral with the parking brake activated. At this point, pause and observe. Reduce noise interference inside the bus, open the windows, and listen. Confirm that a train is neither seen nor heard before crossing the tracks.

Before crossing, ensure that no warning signals are active. If the flashing lights are inactive, the gates are up, and the bells are off, then you may cross. When there is more than one track, cross all at once without stopping. Should any warning signal become active while crossing the tracks, you need to keep going forward. Maintain the same gear throughout the crossing procedure to prevent stalling.

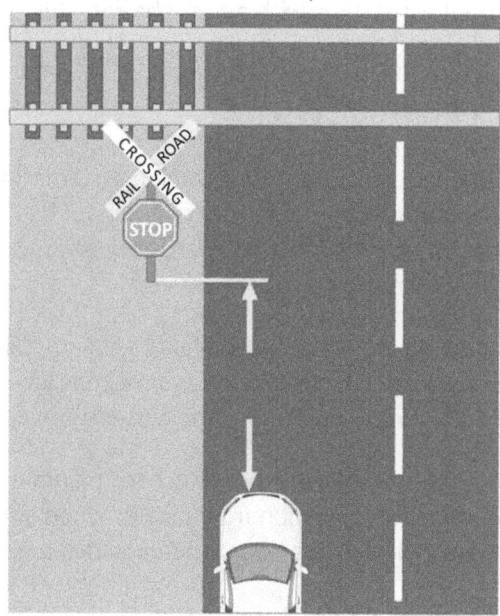

Unique Complications

Some scenarios may present unique complications. If the bus stalls or gets stuck on railroad tracks, you will need to evacuate all passengers and lead them at least 300 feet away from the tracks. Also, when encountering emergency personnel at a crossing site, defer to the instructions of law enforcement agents.

Other complications may occur as the result of natural features in the landscape. Trees, cliffs, and other features may block your view of railroad tracks. You should only cross the railroad tracks if you have a good enough view to determine that the path is clear. Finally, some pathways may be too tight for buses to pass safely through to the other side. Imagine the length of the vehicle doubled, and if that amount of room is unavailable to you on the other side of the tracks, then refrain from proceeding.

Student Management

School bus drivers must occasionally deal with unruly children. While the proper protocol for dealing with misbehaving children may vary based on state or school/district, there are some general guidelines. You must conform to the policies outlined by the school or district for which you drive.

If you must redirect your attention from the road to deal with a problematic passenger, safely bring the bus to a stop in a location where it is not likely to be hit by another vehicle or become susceptible to any other danger. Sometimes, stopping will be sufficient to redirect a misbehaving child, but other times, you may need to leave your seat to speak with the misbehaving child(ren). Whenever you leave your seat to talk with a misbehaving child, turn off the bus and remove the key.

Through training courses and meetings, school districts may equip you with strategies for engaging with unruly children. In general, never yell at or offend misbehaving children, but be firm with them and make it clear that their behavior is unacceptable. You may prompt a child to change his or her seat. You can effectively deter misbehavior by keeping an unruly child close to you. For circumstances that you cannot handle alone, you may request assistance from administrators.

When children misbehave during the loading or unloading process, you must never take your attention away from the children who are entering or exiting the bus. Place all your attention on children entering and exiting the bus. Deal with a misbehaving child or children only after you have completed loading and unloading procedures.

Antilock Braking Systems

Most school buses have antilock braking systems. In the last twenty years, antilock braking systems have been a mandatory feature of every new school bus, and they were installed in most school buses built before that date to meet the standards of newer vehicles. While antilock brakes are an excellent safety feature, they do not replace safe driving.

Antilock braking systems allow drivers to change direction on all surfaces while braking, making it easier to avoid obstacles. Do not take this sometimes life-saving safety feature as an invitation to drive recklessly, however. Antilock braking systems are a last line of defense against serious accidents.

When antilock braking systems are active, maintain pressure on the brake pedal rather than pulse on the brakes. A light on the dashboard indicates when antilock brakes are inactive or not working. Normal brake functions are still available, even when antilock brake systems are inactive.

Special Safety Considerations

You must account for unique scenarios and comprehend specific protocols for safely operating your vehicle in both inclement weather and otherwise. School buses are more affected by inclement weather conditions, like severe winds, than pedestrian vehicles. The size and dimensions of school buses compel drivers to observe specific protocols for maneuvering the vehicle. For example, you should monitor the end of the bus when making turns. Also, you must be prepared to deal with visibility issues in the morning and at other times.

Wind
All vehicles are affected by violent wind gusts, and vehicles traveling at fast speeds feel these effects most severely. Since school buses are more top-heavy than other vehicles, severe winds may force them out of driving lanes or entirely off roads. Severe winds may even knock them over. Maintain control of your bus by firmly holding onto the steering wheel, and, in extreme circumstances, you may benefit from slowing down or pulling over to the side of the road and stopping when you encounter harsh winds. When in doubt about how to proceed, reach out to your supervisors.

Visibility
Fog presents a common visibility issue in the early morning hours. In the winter, the mornings are dark, and you will need to contend with obstructed views. Since roadways are crowded with commuters in the early mornings, you should use the flashing light on the top of the bus as a signal to other drivers. Use these lights in a range of situations, from times when visibility is severely impaired to times when it is only slightly limited. When circumstances require, use these lights in the afternoon and evening as well. Ultimately, defer to state and local guidelines about when to use the top lights.

Backing Up

Finally, the size and dimensions of school buses present challenges when you need to put the bus in reverse. Ordinarily, you should never back up because it is always safer to drive forward with a school bus than backwards. When you have no safer option than to back up, however, ensure that no pedestrians are outside the bus when you do so. If you need to back up at drop-off locations, complete unloading procedures after you have backed up.

When a qualified individual is available, deploy a spotter outside the bus to ensure that no obstacles interfere with the process of backing up. This individual does not tell you how far to back up or in what direction. Instead, this individual's sole responsibility is to alert you if anything gets in the way of the school bus. When a qualified individual is unavailable to fulfill this role—students should not be used as spotters—turn off your engines and apply the parking brake. Then, take the key with you and get out of the bus to check around the outside for obstacles. If the way is clear, complete the process of backing up. As you do so, check the mirrors constantly for any new obstacles.

Practice Quiz

1. Which part of the bus is always dangerous, regardless of how far a student stands from the bus?
    a. Front
    b. Right side
    c. Back
    d. Left side

2. From which part of the bus does the danger zone extend up to 30 feet?
    a. Front
    b. Right side
    c. Back
    d. Left side

3. How far behind the bus should bus drivers be able to see with their outside left- and right-side flat mirrors?
    a. A distance equivalent to the length of four buses
    b. A distance equivalent to the length of two buses
    c. A distance equivalent to the length of twelve buses
    d. A distance equivalent to the length of six buses

4. Which set of mirrors provides a wide view of the areas to either side of a school bus?
    a. Outside left- and right-side flat mirrors
    b. Outside left- and right-side convex mirrors
    c. Outside left- and right-side crossover mirrors
    d. Overhead inside rearview mirror

5. Which set of mirrors provides a view of the front of the bus, over the hood of the bus?
    a. Outside left- and right-side flat mirrors
    b. Outside left- and right-side convex mirrors
    c. Outside left- and right-side crossover mirrors
    d. Overhead inside rearview mirror

Answer Explanations

1. D: Choice *D* is correct because traffic passes on the left side of the bus, so children are always vulnerable to oncoming traffic on the left side. Choice *A* is incorrect because oncoming traffic does not regularly come near the front of the bus. Choice *B* is incorrect because the right side of the bus is protected from oncoming traffic. Choice *C* is incorrect because the rear danger zone extends to a maximum distance of 12 feet.

2. A: Choice *A* is correct because the danger zone in front of the bus extends up to 30 feet from the front bumper. Choices *B* and *C* are incorrect because the danger zones on the right side and in the rear of the bus extend only 12 feet. Choice *D* is incorrect because oncoming traffic is always a danger to children on the left side of the bus, regardless of how far from the bus the children are.

3. A: Choice *A* is correct because drivers should be able to see a distance equivalent to the length of four school buses behind the bus with their flat mirrors. Choice *B* is incorrect because if the mirrors are set to detect any distance less than four bus lengths, then they cannot see far enough. Choice *C* is incorrect because if school bus drivers set their mirrors to see a distance equivalent to the length of twelve school buses, they will not be able to see automobiles directly behind the bus. Choice *D* is incorrect because if school bus drivers set their mirrors to see a distance equivalent to the length of six school buses, they will not be able to see children within the rear danger zone.

4. B: Choice *B* is correct because the convex mirrors provide a wide view of the areas to either side of a school bus. Choice *A* is incorrect because the flat mirrors provide a deep view, rather than a wide view, of the areas to either side of a school bus. Choice *C* is incorrect because the crossover mirrors provide a view from either side across the front of the bus. Choice *D* is incorrect because the rearview mirror provides a view of children inside the bus and vehicles directly behind the bus.

5. C: Choice *C* is correct because the crossover mirrors, from their position on the sides of the bus, provide a view across the front of the bus. Choice *A* is incorrect because the flat mirrors provide a deep view of the areas to either side of a school bus. Choice *B* is incorrect because the convex mirrors provide a wide view of the areas to either side of a school bus. Choice *D* is incorrect because the rearview mirror provides a view of schoolchildren inside the bus and of vehicles directly behind the bus.

Pre-Trip Vehicle Inspection Test

All Vehicles

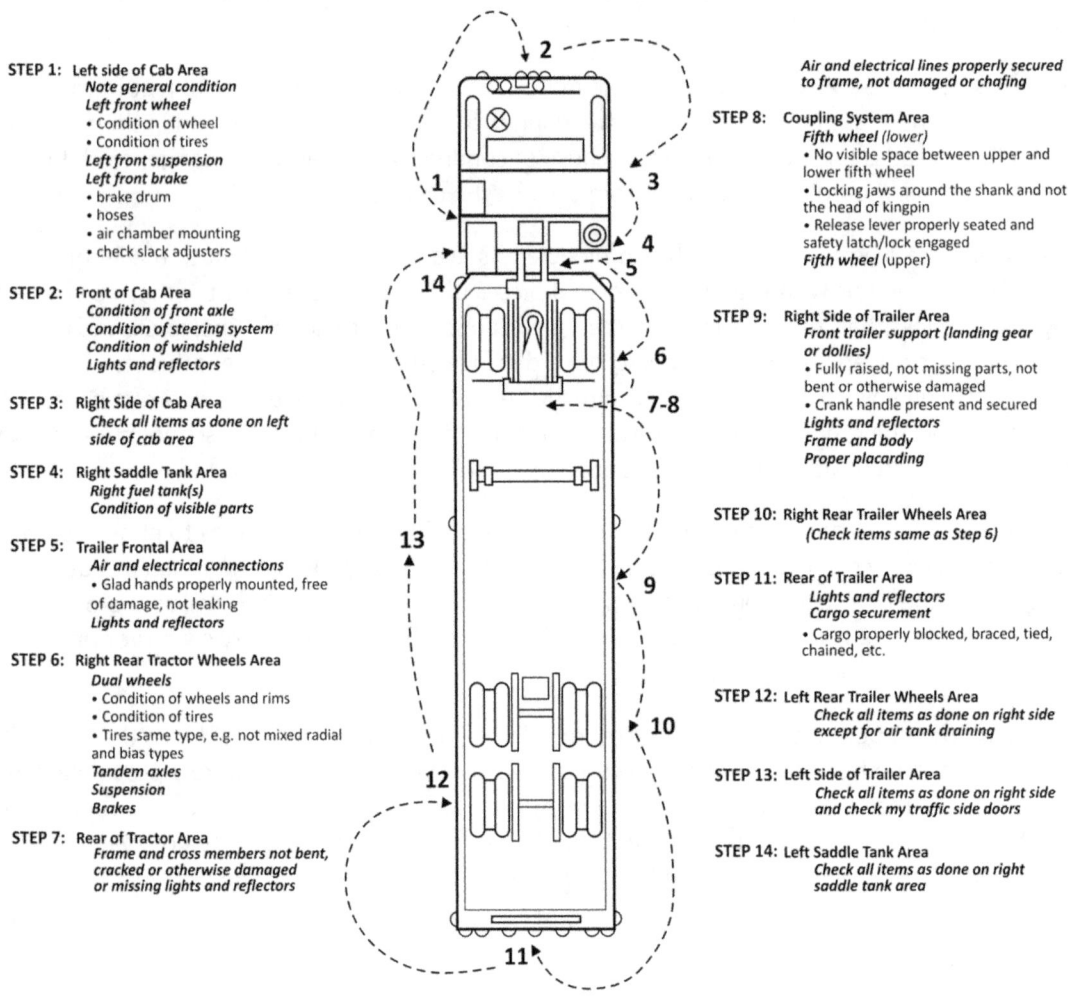

Preliminary Evaluations

During the Vehicle Inspection test, you will be expected to demonstrate knowledge of the various parts of the vehicle and show that they operate correctly. You can prepare for the Vehicle Inspection test by learning about the specific parts that will be tested. You must understand the difference between operable and inoperable parts, and you will need to know how to look for signs that a part of the vehicle is inoperable.

Several factors may indicate that an engine is not working correctly or that operation of the vehicle is suboptimal or dangerous. It is possible to observe many of these signs when the engine is turned off. For example, leaks may indicate a problem with the engine. When liquid accumulates beneath the vehicle, you should check the hoses for signs of wear. You should also assess engine belts for signs of damage, evaluating the tautness of each engine belt and ensuring that none of the belts will soon snap because of degradation over time. Identify all non-belt elements and evaluate their quality as well.

You also need to evaluate the oil level, coolant level, and power steering fluid while the engine is turned off. Evaluate oil level by ensuring that it falls within an acceptable range, meaning that it has not dropped to or below the refill mark. Evaluate the coolant level by determining whether it correctly fits the gauge or that it passes the eye test for acceptability. Likewise, measure power steering fluid by ensuring that its quantity has not dropped to or below the refill mark.

Test Start

Once you complete these preliminary evaluations, make sure the vehicle starts correctly by completing a test start. Completing a test start is no different than how you would start the vehicle in non-test settings.

If you drive a vehicle with automatic transmission, put it in park and turn the engine on. If you drive a vehicle with standard transmission, put it in neutral, activate the clutch, and turn the engine on. Maintain pressure on the clutch until the engine reaches a comfortable resting speed. Then remove pressure from the clutch. Listen to the sound of the engine and evaluate whether the engine runs effectively.

Gauge Evaluations with Engine Activated

Once you activate the engine, turn your attention to important indicators inside the cabin. You will know that the oil pressure gauge works when it records standard values or when it indicates that oil pressure values are increasing toward normal values. The oil pressure warning light should, of course, deactivate when the engine is turned on. The temperature gauge works like the oil pressure gauge, so you can evaluate its function by ensuring that it records normal temperature levels or that temperature levels ascend toward acceptable levels.

While you should evaluate both the ammeter and voltmeter like you evaluate the oil pressure and temperature gauges, you will need to read the air gauge a bit differently. When you evaluate the ammeter and voltmeter, ensure that power increases in both the alternator and the generator. In contrast, look for specific readings from the air gauge. Generally, you want to see that the air pressure exceeds 119 pounds of force per square inch of area (psi), and that it remains below 141 psi.

Equipment Evaluations with Engine Activated

Since safety depends on visibility, you should closely monitor the integrity of your windshields and mirrors. Ensure that these surfaces are clean and set your mirrors to optimize ability to see around all sides of the bus. Nothing should block your view through the windshield. You can inspect windshield wipers and washers simultaneously. Ensure that wipers work properly and that they are adequately attached.

You will also evaluate the lights, turn signals, and other important mechanisms inside the cabin. Test the left and right turn signals, headlights, and emergency lights. Turn them on and then back off again to ensure proper function. Ensure that the outside lights are not discolored or dirty in a way that might affect visibility. Check all clearance lights, brake lights, backing lights, taillights, and flashers. Although clearance lights are amber on most parts of the vehicle, clearance lights located on the back of the vehicle are red. The same rule applies for all reflectors. You also need to check the antilock braking system by identifying its signal on the dashboard. Finally, test the horn, heater, and defroster.

In addition to assessing the function of all mechanisms, check for required safety equipment. Ensure that a fire extinguisher is present and that it is both ready for use and properly secured. Ensure the presence of flares, fuses, and reflective traffic signals. Immediately note the absence of fuses to test administrators. Then ensure the integrity of safety belts.

Evaluating the Brakes

There are several types of brake systems within a CMV; you will need to evaluate the functioning of all systems. Ensure that brake systems work correctly and show no sign of disrepair.

Parking brakes prevent vehicles from moving when they are in park. Evaluate their function by trying to move the vehicle while the parking brake is active. Parking brakes should prevent the vehicle from moving.

For combination vehicles—those with a separate parking brake for the cabin and the trailer—you should complete two tests. First, activate the cabin parking brake but deactivate the trailer parking brake. Accelerate gently to see if the vehicle moves. Second, deactivate the cabin parking brake but activate the trailer parking brake. Again, accelerate gently to see if the vehicle moves.

Test the service brakes by slowly moving the vehicle forward and applying the brakes. Ensure that the vehicle stops and that it does not veer to either side when you apply the brakes. If the vehicle fulfills both criteria, then the service brakes are operable.

Test the hydraulic brake systems a bit differently than the way you test the parking brakes and service brakes. You must ensure that the hydraulic brake system is active by pushing the brake pedal down three times then maintaining pressure on the brake pedal for five seconds; if the brake pedal does not descend during that time, then the test is complete. Additionally, test the hydraulic brake reserve system by holding pressure. Listen for the sound of the reserve motor. Finally, ensure that the hydraulic brake system reserve light is inactive.

Properly evaluating the air brakes is one of the most important steps in the Vehicle Inspection test. Drivers who are unable to complete any of the three parts of the air brake assessment receive an automatic failing mark on the Vehicle Inspection test. Using the correct procedures for evaluating air brakes is crucial. Begin this stage of the Vehicle Inspection test by raising the air pressure to the ideal range, between 120 and 140 psi. Then, turn the engine off and leave the key in position. Disengage the parking brake and the protection valve simultaneously, then press the foot brake for one minute. With a single vehicle, observe if the air pressure decreases by a rate greater than three pounds per minute; with a combination vehicle, observe if air pressure decreases by a rate greater than four pounds per minute. Next, swiftly engage and disengage the foot brake. Ensure that alert mechanisms activate when air pressure reaches a point lower than that specified by the vehicle's owner manual. Finally, continue to

Pre-Trip Vehicle Inspection Test

engage and disengage the foot brake until air pressure reaches a point where the tractor protection valve and parking brake release.

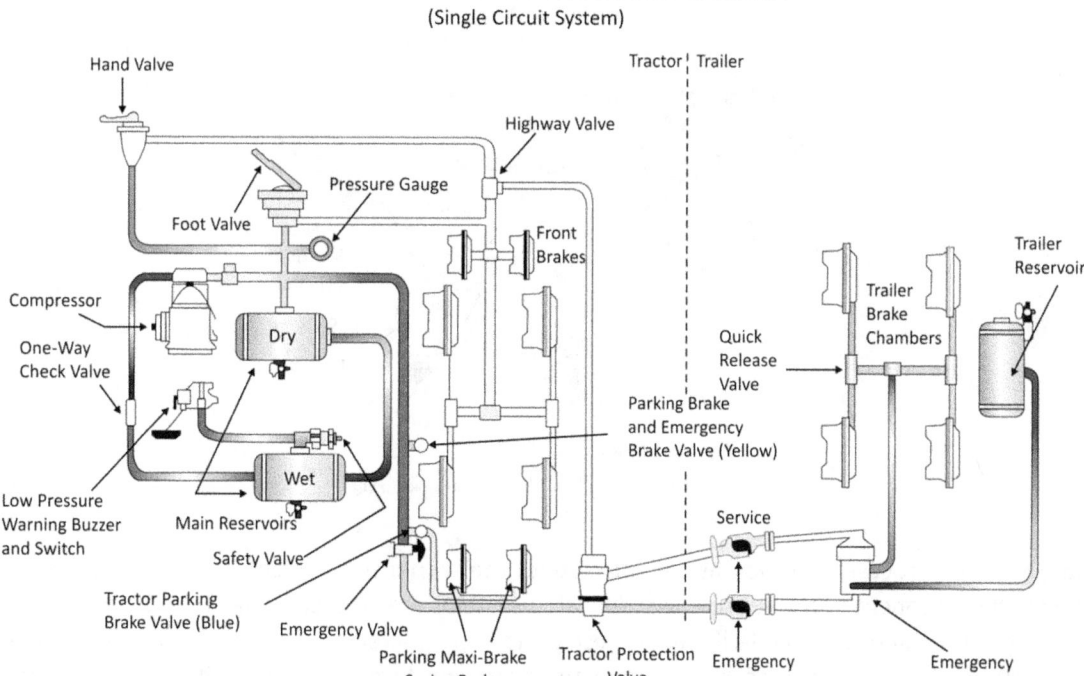

External Inspection (All Vehicles)

Steering System and Suspension System

You ensure the integrity of numerous parts of the vehicle when you complete an external inspection. Starting with the steering system, ensure that the steering box is fastened in its place and all parts are attached. Additionally, assess the status of the power steering hoses. Survey the area under power steering hoses for signs of discharge and check each hose for signs of corruption. Ensure that the steering box and steering hoses are functional.

You must ensure the integrity of a third element of the steering system: steering linkage. Ensure that component parts are connected, that all parts are present, and that these parts are in good working order.

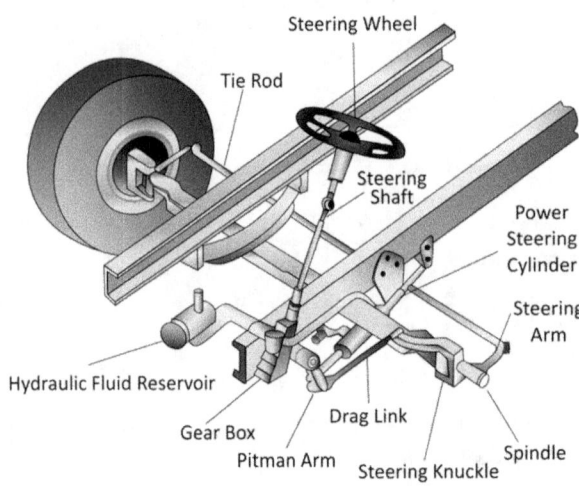

Complete a similar process when you assess the state of the suspension system. You must ensure the integrity of all component parts, but not all suspension systems are created equal. First, assess the status of leaf springs and coil springs. Note if any of these parts are impaired or missing. Then check to see if the vehicle is equipped with other parts, like torsion bars. If the vehicle is equipped with these parts, then ensure that they are installed properly and in good working order. Otherwise, review the air ride suspension for signs of degradation.

Mounts tend to shake loose from their places, so check for displaced or misplaced parts. Complete this process for every point along the structure of the vehicle where mounts connect to either an axle or a part of the vehicle's frame. You must ensure that mounts are secure.

The process used to check shock absorbers resembles the process used to check mounts. Over time, shock absorbers wear down and may become compromised. Ensure that shock absorbers are fastened in place and that no discharge is present. Complete this assessment for every axle on the vehicle, including those on attached, unpowered vehicles, like trailers, and on the tractor (the "head" of the truck).

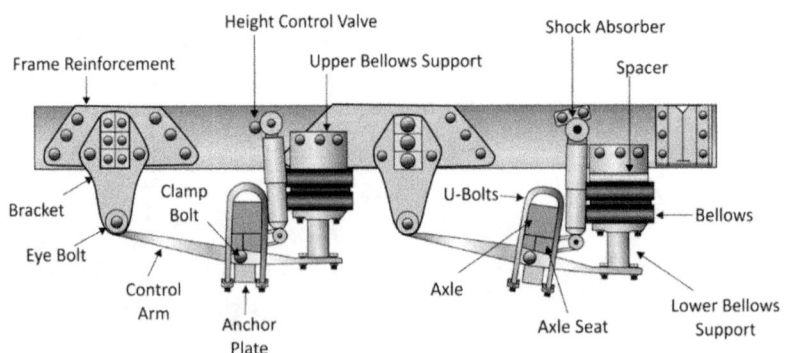

Brakes and Wheels

While proper inspections of brakes and wheels are two distinct phases of the external inspection portion of the Vehicle Inspection test, these phases are similar in that you must complete thorough inspections of component parts. Check for familiar signs of deterioration and instability, relative to the examined part. These signs differ depending on the part of the vehicle that you check, so drivers should be familiar with the common signs of deterioration and instability that apply to each part.

Evaluate slack adjustors and pushrods by ensuring the integrity of these parts and checking that all pieces are both present and properly connected. On vehicles with manual transmissions, evaluate the brake pushrod by pulling it while the brakes are disengaged. Under these conditions, the brake pushrod should not move a distance greater than one inch from its starting point.

Evaluate the integrity of brake chambers and ensure that all parts are present and properly connected. Follow this same procedure when you check brake hoses and lines. Additionally, check for discharge around these areas.

You may evaluate the drum brake and brake linings simultaneously. Beginning with the drum brake, ensure the integrity of this mechanism and ensure that all parts are both present and properly connected. You should also ensure that drum brakes are not coated with an excess of lubricating substances, like grease, and that drum brakes are clean. Since brake linings wear out over time, ensure that the brake lining material is both thick and strong. Additionally, you should notice whether it is possible to see brake linings through the drum brakes on the vehicle you inspect. If there are openings through which you can see through the drum brakes to the brake linings, then ensure that a portion of the brake lining appears in this opening. This eye test ensures that brake linings are in place. Complete this process for every drum brake on the vehicle, including attached vehicles, like trailers and cabins.

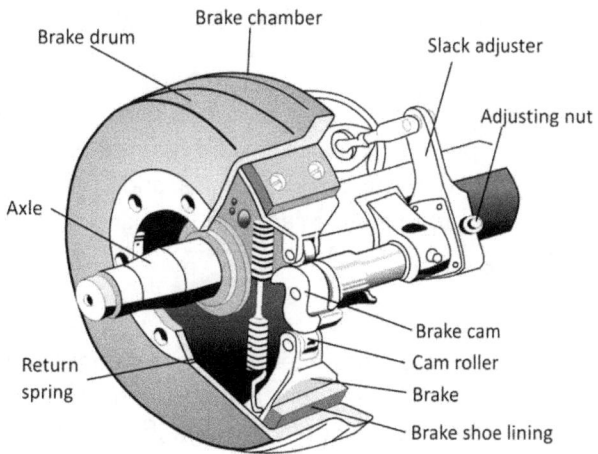

Like the component parts of the brakes, you should evaluate nuances when you inspect the component parts of the wheels. Ensure the integrity of the wheels by searching for fractures along the rim structure. Rim damage should not be fixed via welding, so ensure that the rims do not show any sign of having been welded. Look for rust along the rim, which may be a sign that the rim is not properly secured to the wheel.

You will need to evaluate several factors related to the integrity of tires. Ensure that all tires, except tires on the steering axle, have a minimum tread depth of 1/16, and that tires on the steering axle have a minimum tread depth of 2/16. Each tire should not be in a state of disrepair or decay. Ensure that each tire is strong and fresh. Ensure that stems and valve caps are both present and properly installed. Apply a similar level of rigor when you evaluate tire inflation. Tires should not be checked in an unscrupulous manner, simply by touching them; instead, evaluate tire inflation with tire gauge.

When you evaluate hub oil seals and axle seals, ensure that no discharge is present around these areas and that oil ascends to a functional level. Ensure that no lug nuts are missing, that they are in good condition, and that every lug nut is tight in its fixture. Finally, ensure that spacers are in good condition and placed centrally in dual tires. Ensure balanced spacing between dual tires and repeat this process for every wheel on the vehicle, including wheels on unpowered vehicles and tractors.

Side and Rear of Vehicles

Vehicles' outsides endure a substantial amount of wear and tear over time. You must ensure the integrity of various parts along the side and back of vehicles as well as the presence of all pieces belonging to each part.

Doors and mirrors ensure the safety of drivers, passengers, and other vehicles on the road. You need to check that doors and mirrors operate correctly and are in good condition. You and your passengers must be able to enter and exit the vehicle without an issue. Doors should not show signs of severe damage. Make sure that door hinges are fastened and mirrors are fastened on both sides of the vehicle.

Once you evaluate the doors and mirrors, assess the fuel tank, drive shaft, exhaust system, and frame for signs of structural damage and loose fixtures. Ensure that the fuel tank is fastened in its place, that the fuel cap is tight, and that there are no signs of discharge around that part of the vehicle. Assess the integrity of the drive shaft by ensuring that all component parts are present and connected. Additionally, ensure that no alien parts are present. When you evaluate the exhaust system, look for signs of rust and carbon discharge. Note buildup of these properties. Ensure that the exhaust system is fastened in place. Finally, ensure that the vehicle's frame is in good condition, without signs of meaningful damage, and that all component parts are present.

At the rear of the vehicle, check to see if splash guards or mud flaps are present. If they are, ensure that they are in good condition and are fastened in place. Ensure that the rear doors are in good working condition and fastened correctly. Also, ensure that ties, chains, and other bindings connect. Finally, demonstrate your knowledge of how to operate a cargo lift by taking it off and reinstalling it. Also check the cargo lift for signs of discharge.

Tractor and Shaft Coupling

Pay close attention to the area around the fifth wheel and the component parts related to maintaining the integrity of the structure. Evaluate the mounting bolts and ensure that the slide mounting and the fifth wheel are fastened. Additionally, observe the kingpin, through the fifth wheel gap, to ensure that locking jaws surround the kingpin. Ensure that the locking jaws are fastened to each respective part. Furthermore, ensure that the fifth wheel skid plate is properly maintained, that it is fastened to the platform, and that all parts are present. Inspect the fifth wheel platform for signs of wear and tear. This platform is essential to the integrity of the fifth wheel skid plate. Finally, ensure that the fifth wheel release arm is both properly positioned and working. Note that not all vehicles are equipped with a fifth wheel release arm or fifth wheel locking pins; when locking pins are present, ensure that they are all present. When these components are air powered, ensure that the system is secured, without leaks.

In addition to closely inspecting the area around the fifth wheel, you should ensure the integrity of air and electric lines by checking for leaks, frays, and entanglements. None of the electric or air lines should interfere with other parts of the tractor. You should not be able to see the steel interior inside electric lines.

You must also ensure the integrity of structurally supportive elements by checking that catwalks and catwalk steps are both fastened and durable. Additionally, ensure that the hitch release lever is both present and fastened. Ensure that all parts of the sliding pintle, tongue, drawbar, and tongue storage area are present and in good condition.

School Bus Only

You will need to assess several features, both inside and outside the vehicle, to ensure proper function and safety. Since passenger safety is a significant concern, you must ensure the presence and proper function of everything from emergency equipment to seating. Furthermore, you must understand the proper procedures for checking this equipment.

During preliminary checks of emergency equipment, ensure the presence of reflectors. School buses should have either three red reflective triangles, six fusees (a match-like type of flare), or three liquid-burning flares. Additionally, you must ensure that fire extinguishers are present, in place, and properly charged. Finally, ensure the presence of an emergency first aid kit, as well as a kit for properly cleaning bodily excrements, like blood and urine.

Lighting Indicators, Lights, and Reflectors
As its name suggests, lighting indicators tell drivers when flashing amber lights, alternately flashing red lights, and/or strobe lights are activated. Flashing amber lights indicators and strobe lights indicators are not present on every school bus vehicle, but when they are, you should ensure that both indicators function. Since alternately flashing red lights are present on every school bus vehicle, you will always need to ensure their proper functioning.

Lights and lighting indicators correspond to one another, so when certain lights are absent from a bus, the indicators for those lights are also absent. The red lights on the front and back of the bus are always present on school buses, so you should always ensure that they function correctly. Strobe lights, stop arm lights, and alternately flashing amber lights are not present on every school bus vehicle, but when they are, you will need to ensure that they function correctly.

Students Entering the School Bus Safely
You will need to examine features related to student safety while entering the school bus. Ensure that the stop arm, also known as the safety arm, fully opens when operated, and ensure that it is in good working condition. Ensure that the entry path is clear; the door closes appropriately; handrails are durable, reliable, and fastened in place; and the step light is operational. Finally, assess the integrity of the handicap lift, and demonstrate competency by uninstalling and reinstalling it.

Student Safety Inside the Bus
Student mirrors, emergency exits, and seating help to ensure student safety. You will need to assess these fixtures for signs of wear and tear. Ensure that student mirrors provide a clear view of passengers, are positioned in the correct place, and are fastened properly. Additionally, ensure that these surfaces are clean and that your vision is unimpeded. Since the emergency exit allows students to flee the school bus in times of distress, ensure that these exits are operational and that they may be opened from inside and

outside the bus. During the Vehicle Inspection Tests, you must identify each emergency exit and explain how to operate them. Ensure that caution signals correspond to each emergency exit appropriately when each emergency exit is engaged. Finally, ensure that each seat is fastened to the floor and that the cushions of every seat are fastened to their frames.

Trailer

You may complete an assessment of both the vehicle's and the trailer's suspension system, wheels, brakes, and splash guard simultaneously.

Evaluate the suspension systems by identifying their nuances. Check for missing parts and additional parts and identify whether the trailer has an air ride suspension system.

Follow the same procedures for evaluating the slack adjustors, pushrods, brake chambers, drum brakes, and brake linings of the trailers as you do when you adjust these features of their brakes and wheel systems. Ensure the integrity of these component parts and pay close attention to the nuances of each part.

Trailer Unique Features

Vehicles and trailers share many of the same features, but trailers do have certain unique features. In the front of the trailer, you will find air connectors, glad hands, and electrical plugs. These features are known as the trailer's air or electrical connections. Ensure that the glad hands do not leak and are in their proper position. The trailer air connectors and electrical plugs also need to be secured and in good shape.

Some trailers have header boards, which often carry large quantities of heavy items. When header boards are present, ensure that they are equipped to handle large quantities of various materials. When protective covers accompany header boards, ensure that these covers are in their proper position. Drivers of enclosed trailers ensure their integrity by assessing signs of wear and tear, especially at the front of the trailer.

Along the side of the trailer, evaluate landing gear, doors, ties, and lifts, as well as the trailer's frame. Ensure that the trailer's frame is durable and that it suffered no signs of significant wear and tear. When applicable, ensure that both the tandem release arm and locking pins are present and fastened to their zone. You must ensure that doors open from outside the vehicle. Additionally, when the vehicle is equipped with a cargo lift, demonstrate competency by checking for leaks and uninstalling and reinstalling this feature. Finally, assess landing gear by ensuring that all component parts are in good condition and that landing gear idles at its highest point. When landing gear is power operated, check for signs of discharge.

Coach/Transit Bus

To ensure the safety of their passengers, coach and transit bus drivers must properly assess both the inside and outside of their vehicle.

Internal Factors

Ensuring that passengers make it safely onto the vehicle is your first safety concern as a driver. When completing the internal inspection of their vehicle, ensure that entry doors function properly and can be pulled closed from inside the vehicle. There should be no gaps between the door and the door frame when the entry door is closed. You will also need to inspect the entryway. Ensure that entryways are clear and that the flooring is fresh and not terribly worn down. Test handrails to ensure that they are fastened.

Finally, demonstrate competency of handicap lifts by articulating the proper steps to evaluate it and by uninstalling and reinstalling the lifts. Ensure that all parts of the handicap lift are present and that lifts are in good working order, without sign of hazardous discharge.

Ensure that you can pull all emergency doors closed from the inside. Check these doors for signs of wear and tear and ensure that emergency warning indicators function. Ensure that all doors and mirrors are in good condition and fastened correctly to their positions.

Finally, ensure the proper set-up of passenger seats. Ensure that seat frames are both in good condition and fastened to the floor. Additionally, ensure that seat cushions are fastened to seat frames. These precautions prevent accidents and help ensure passenger safety.

External Factors

You will need to evaluate several factors outside the vehicle for signs of damage or decay. Ensure that the suspension system has no significant issues by checking that all parts of the vehicle sit evenly on the ground. Assess the suspension system by listening for leaks. Ensure that fuel tanks are fastened in place and the tanks are not leaking.

Check the integrity of the baggage compartments and the battery box. Additionally, ensure that the batteries have a good connection. Note the presence of cell caps and evaluate batteries for signs of decay.

Taking the CDL Vehicle Inspection Test

The CDL Vehicle Inspection Test is broken into two categories, according to the kind of license sought. The first category pertains to the inspection of Class A vehicles, and the second category pertains to the inspection of Class B and C vehicles. The main difference between these two categories is that Class B and C vehicles include passenger vehicles like school buses and coach buses.

There are four versions of the Class A Vehicle Inspection Test and three versions of the Class B and C Vehicle Inspection Test. You will take just one version of the Class A, B, or C tests. Test instructors decide which version of the test each driver takes; you will not know ahead of time which version of the test you will take.

All four versions of the Class A test share four common features: an engine start assessment, an in-cab inspection, a coupling system inspection, and either a total vehicle inspection or an inspection of one specific area of the vehicle.

All three versions of the Class B and C tests share three common features: an engine start assessment; an in-cab inspection; a total vehicle inspection or an inspection of one specific area of the vehicle; and an inspection related to the type of vehicle they drive. For example, of school bus drivers complete an inspection of a unique feature of school buses, and coach bus drivers complete an inspection of a unique feature of coach buses.

Practice Quiz

1. The air gauge should record air pressure measurements within which range?
    a. 100-120 psi
    b. 110-130 psi
    c. 120-140 psi
    d. 130-150psi

2. Which color should clearance lights on the back of the vehicle be?
    a. Red
    b. Amber
    c. Orange
    d. Yellow

3. Not counting the back of the vehicle, which color should reflectors on all the other parts of the vehicle be?
    a. Red
    b. Amber
    c. Orange
    d. Yellow

4. Which missing component should drivers tell examiners about?
    a. Liquid-burning flares
    b. Red reflective triangles
    c. Electrical fuses
    d. Fire extinguisher

5. Failure to complete any step of which of the following brake assessments leads to an automatic failure of the Vehicle Inspection Test?
    a. Service brake check
    b. Parking brake check
    c. Hydraulic brake check
    d. Air brake check

Answer Explanations

1. C: Choice *C* is correct because air pressure measurements should fall within the range of 120 to 140 psi. Choice *A* is incorrect because these air pressure measurements are too low, apart from the one measurement at the top of the range (120 psi). Choice *B* is incorrect because, while air pressure measurements from 120 to 130 are acceptable, air pressure measurements from 110 to 119 are too low. Choice *D* is incorrect because, while air pressure measurements from 130 to 140 are acceptable, air pressure measurements from 141 to 150 are too high.

2. A: Choice *A* is correct because clearance lights on the back of the vehicle should be red. Choice *B* is incorrect because, while clearance lights on other parts of the vehicle are amber, clearance lights on the back of the vehicle are red. Choices *C* and *D* are incorrect because clearance lights are not orange or yellow.

3. B: Choice *B* is correct because reflectors on all parts of the vehicle except the back are amber. Choice *A* is incorrect because, while reflectors on the back of the vehicle are red, reflectors on all other parts of the vehicle are amber. Choices *C* and *D* are incorrect because reflectors are not orange or yellow.

4. C: Choice *C* is correct because drivers must notify test examiners when electrical fuses are missing. Choices *A* and *B* are incorrect because just one of these components is required, either liquid-burning flares or reflective triangles. Choice *D* is incorrect because drivers do not have to notify examiners if fire extinguishers are missing.

5. D: Choice *D* is correct because failure to complete any step of the air brake assessment results in automatic failure of the Vehicle Inspection Test. Choices *A, B, C* are incorrect because failure to complete any step of the parking brake, service brake, or hydraulic brake assessment does not necessarily result in failure.

Basic Vehicle Control Skills Test

Scoring

There are plenty of ways to lose points on the Vehicle Control Skills Test. You should know how you might lose points on the test and prepare to avoid penalties. Focus on limiting the number of outside vehicle observations you complete during the test and executing them looks properly. Be familiar with encroachments and pull-ups and know how to avoid these penalties as well.

The Vehicle Control Skills Test will require you to complete complicated maneuvers with grace and finesse. You will be required to end each maneuver precisely where examiners instruct. You may fail the skill test if you do not end the maneuvers in the spot dictated by the examiner.

It is common for drivers to have a good sense of where their vehicle is in relation to other objects on the road or test course, but then lose awareness as the exam progresses. To gain better vision of obstacles around the vehicle, you may complete outside vehicle observations by getting out of the vehicle to check the surroundings.

An outside vehicle observation ("look") is an acceptable way to gain knowledge about a vehicle's location and the environment. You are only allowed a certain number of looks per maneuver, however. For most maneuvers, you are allowed two looks. For the Straight-Line Backing maneuver, however, you are allowed only one look.

To properly complete a look, first put the vehicle in neutral and apply the parking brake. Next, leave the vehicle while keeping three points of contact. Keep a strong grip on the handrails as you dismount. Failure to exit the vehicle properly may lead to an instant failure.

Use looks tactfully throughout the test to avoid encroachments. When you touch or pass over a line of demarcation, that is called an encroachment. Encroachments incur penalties in the Vehicle Control Skills Test.

Try to avoid encroachments by carefully navigating around demarcated lines. When you stop the vehicle and change direction to avoid an encroachment, however, you might be penalized for an illegal pull-up. Penalties for pull-ups stack over time. You will not be penalized at first, but too many pull-ups will count against you.

Exercises

The Basic Vehicle Control Skills Test consists of several exercises that emulate standard on-road maneuvers. Straight Line Backing and Parallel Parking are included in the list of exercises that you will complete on the Basic Vehicle Control Skills Test. Prepare for this test by familiarizing yourself with the full list of testable exercises.

The Straight-Line Backing exercise will require you to successfully drive your vehicle backward, without diverging too far from a straight path. Cones are arranged in two straight, parallel lines. With the vehicle in reverse, you will maneuver between these lines. You will receive penalties for crossing the lines with the vehicle or interfering with the cones in any way.

Two parking exercises will also require you to successfully maneuver with the vehicle in reverse. The Offset Back/Right and Offset Back/Left exercises will require you to back into a parking spot to the left or right of

Basic Vehicle Control Skills Test

the vehicle. Complete these exercises by first driving beyond the parking spot and then backing into the opposite lane. Once you clear the boundary with the front of the vehicle, put the vehicle in park.

Parallel Parking exercises feature prominently on the Basic Vehicle Control Skills Test. You will complete one Parallel Parking exercise on the left side of the vehicle and another on the right side. Follow the same steps to complete both Parallel Parking exercises. You will receive penalties for crossing boundary lines with the vehicle and for leaving parts of the vehicle exposed to traffic.

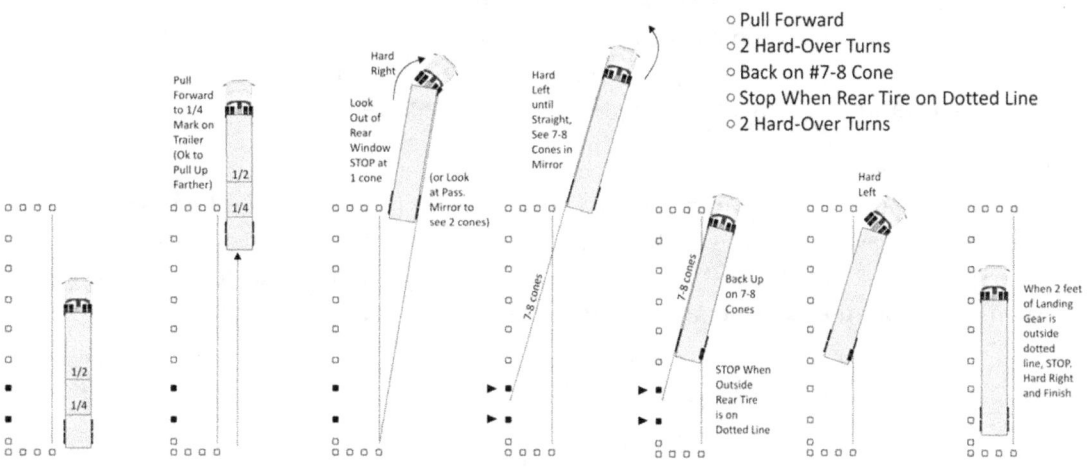

Finally, the Alley Dock exercise will require you to use skills from previous exercises to complete a tricky maneuver. As its name suggests, the Alley Dock exercise simulates the experience of backing a vehicle into an alley. Not only must you back the vehicle between two parallel rows without crossing either boundary line, but you must also complete a near-90-degree-turn into rows of cones representing an alley. Complete this exercise by stopping the vehicle three feet from the back of the alley.

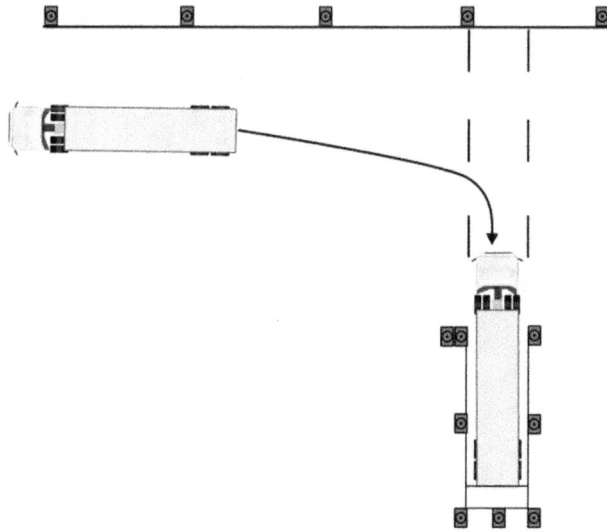

Practice Quiz

1. What counts as an encroachment?
    a. Any time drivers touch or cross over the boundary line
    b. Any time drivers touch or cross over the boundary line without correction
    c. Any time drivers proceed from one exercise to another without signaling
    d. Any time drivers fail to follow the examiner's instructions

2. What counts as a pull-up?
    a. Any time drivers pass an encroachment without touching it
    b. Any time drivers pull beyond a parking spot to parallel park
    c. Any time drivers stop and then reposition to clear an encroachment
    d. Any time drivers fail to come to a complete stop at an intersection

3. What counts as a look?
    a. When drivers adjust their mirrors to gain a better view while the test is in progress
    b. When drivers leave the vehicle to check the position of the vehicle from outside
    c. When drivers look both ways at intersections and signal the right of way to oncoming traffic
    d. When drivers use the examiner as a spotter to direct their maneuvers while in reverse

Answer Explanations

1. A: Choice *A* is correct because an encroachment occurs whenever a driver's vehicle touches or crosses over a boundary line. Choice *B* is incorrect because encroachments are not "forgiven" if a driver corrects the mistake. Choice *C* is incorrect because drivers do not move from one exercise to another at their own pace. Choice *D* is incorrect because failing to follow an examiner's instructions does not count as an encroachment.

2. C: Choice *C* is correct because pull-ups are defined in relation to encroachments. Drivers use pull-ups to avoid committing an encroachment. Choice *A* is incorrect because it suggests that encroachments are objects on the exam course. Choice *B* is incorrect because, while a driver may do a pull-up to avoid passing incorrectly through a parking spot, pull-ups are not a necessary part of parallel parking. Choice *D* is incorrect because pull-ups have nothing to do with safely stopping at intersections.

3. B: Choice *B* is correct because a look occurs when drivers get out of the vehicle to gain a better view of the vehicle's position. Choice *A* is incorrect because looks do not have to do with a vehicle's mirrors. Choice *C* is incorrect because looks do not have to do with safely passing through intersections. Choice *D* is incorrect because looks and spotters are not related to one another.

On-Road Driving

How You Will Be Tested

Prepare to Turn

The on-road driving portion of the test will require you to respond to prompts. The examiner will prompt you to make turns, and you must do so while conforming to proper turning procedures. The examiner will prompt you to turn well enough in advance so that you have time to prepare. You should complete two steps to prepare for each turn: evaluate traffic in all lanes, then merge into the lane where you will make their turn.

Use either their right or left turn signal as you get closer to the turn. Decelerate and avoid coasting in neutral for a prolonged period. Sometimes, you must come to a stop before completing a turn. When circumstances require this, you must stop before any road markings at the intersection. Maintain a safe distance behind the vehicle in front of you. A safe distance allows you to see the back tires of the vehicle in front of you.

Make the Turn

Avoid turning your wheels prematurely. Only once you begin the turn should you start turning the steering wheel. Turn slowly and carefully to avoid making mistakes.

End the turn in the same lane of traffic that you turned into. Ensure precision by checking your mirrors for obstacles. Keep both hands on the steering wheel to ensure full control of the vehicle. Never veer outside of the turning lane into other lanes of traffic.

The examiner will evaluate your ability to merge with the speed of traffic. You must not make yourself a hazard to other vehicles by either slowing down the flow of traffic or presenting the vehicle as an obstacle. Use your turn signals to merge into the right lane of traffic. Maintain consistency and control by checking your mirrors for obstacles and traffic.

Approaching and Passing Intersections

The process for navigating intersections resembles the process for completing a turn, even if you are not completing a turn at the intersection. Evaluate traffic and slow down the vehicle. Avoid coasting, and, if you must stop, bring the vehicle to a complete stop. At that point, ensure that the vehicle does not move from its stationary position.

Even if you do not have to stop at a particular intersection, you still must slow down. Vehicles and pedestrians frequently attempt to cross intersections, and you must yield appropriately. Scrupulously evaluate traffic, keep your hands on the steering wheel, and never change lanes in an intersection. After passing through the intersection, reevaluate traffic and accelerate to its speed.

Stop and Start

At some point during the on-road driving test, the examiner will prompt you to complete a successful start and stop, according to pertinent safety guidelines. Bring the vehicle to a stop and use the turn signal to indicate your intention to move to the side of the road. Evaluate traffic and come to a complete stop without coasting. Ensure that the vehicle stops parallel to the road and out of the way of traffic. Do not stop in the way of intersections, driveways, or fire hydrants. Replace your turn signal with emergency lights. Finally, apply the parking brake and remove your feet from the brake and clutch.

After a while, the examiner will prompt you to restart the vehicle and rejoin the flow of traffic. Replace the emergency lights with the left turn signal. Evaluate traffic in all directions and merge into the right lane when the coast is clear. Use the steering wheel to merge into traffic once the vehicle is already in motion.

Special Considerations

Complete special procedures when approaching or navigating curves, lane changes, expressways, and urban business areas. Approach curves with caution by decelerating to maintain control of the vehicle and avoid oncoming traffic. Evaluate traffic in both directions.

Maintain a similar level of rigor when merging onto and off expressways. Signal and evaluate traffic. When merging onto expressways, accelerate to the speed of traffic and maintain a safe distance in relation to other vehicles. When exiting expressways, decelerate and maintain proper space between your vehicle and other vehicles on the exit ramp.

Make lane changes both as necessary and when prompted by the examiner. When prompted by the examiner to make a lane change, merge from one lane to another after signaling with your turn signal and evaluating traffic.

In urban business areas, maintain a speed that corresponds with surrounding traffic, without going faster than the speed limit. Constantly evaluate traffic, stay to the right of traffic, and maintain a safe distance between your vehicle and other vehicles.

Railroad Crossings

Railroad crossing procedures for drivers of passenger vehicles are more extensive than those for drivers of commercial vehicles. This section only covers railroad crossing procedures for drivers of commercial vehicles. Information about railroad crossing procedures for drivers of passenger vehicles is found in the school buses section. In some states, commercial drivers may need to follow railroad crossing procedures for drivers of passenger vehicles. Be sure to consult local state procedures for further information.

Slow down when approaching railroad crossings and bring the vehicle to a complete stop. Evaluate the railroad for signs of an approaching train and yield to activated railroad crossing signs. Finally, evaluate all traffic and move over railroad crossing sites without stopping, changing lanes, or passing other vehicles.

Other Considerations

Any traffic sign that you pass during the on-road test is fair game for evaluation. Be sure to pay attention to all signs you pass because the examiner will likely ask you to describe road signs after you have already passed them.

You must constantly evaluate traffic, especially at intersections and in congested areas. Always steer deliberately and forcefully, with two hands on the wheel. Take a hand off the wheel only to shift gears. Stay in the right lane unless for some reason you are unable to gain access to the right lane. Stay within lane markings and finish turns in the intended lane.

Use your brakes and turn signals according to proper procedures. Never stop abruptly at intersections or railroad crossings. Instead, bring the vehicle to a stop gradually. Never drive with your foot on the brake pedal or pump the brakes. Signal early and often with turn signals every time you turn or change lanes. Promptly stop using your turn signals once you complete the intended maneuver.

Considerations for Drivers of Manual Vehicles

Drivers of manual vehicles must follow specific procedures for both gear usage and clutch usage. Never do anything to cause gear abrasion. Do not shift or select gears that may cause the piston rings to break. Additionally, always shift gears with the clutch, and double clutch when you drive a vehicle with an unsynchronized engine. Use the clutch exclusively to change gears.

Practice Test

1. Which parking position is recommended for CMV drivers?
    a. Parking in a spot that can be pulled through
    b. Parking closely to other vehicles
    c. Backing into a parking space on the side of the road
    d. Always parking downhill on a curve

2. What is the first step drivers should take before backing up?
    a. Put the truck in the lowest gear.
    b. Ask someone to stand behind the truck and guide them.
    c. Make sure cargo is securely in place.
    d. Inspect mirrors for cleanliness, line of vision, and to make sure there's nothing behind them.

3. What is the *last* step a driver should take when shifting to a higher gear?
    a. Shift into neutral.
    b. Allow the engine to slow down.
    c. Push the accelerator and let go of the clutch.
    d. Shift to a higher gear and push the clutch.

4. What is the first thing you should try to do when encountering fog?
    a. Keep driving and turn on the low beams.
    b. Find a safe place to pull over and wait it out.
    c. Turn on the high beams and speed through it.
    d. Turn around and go a different way.

5. Complete the following statement: When driving 40 mph, the driver should leave one second of space for every _____ feet of vehicle length.
    a. 20
    b. 15
    c. 5
    d. 10

6. Which of the following is NOT a common distraction while driving?
    a. Calculating stopping distance
    b. Talking over the dispatcher
    c. Adjusting the mirrors
    d. Having a negative temperament

7. Which of the following is a sign that another driver might be impaired?
    a. They flash their high beams.
    b. They are talking on a cell phone.
    c. They weave in and out of a lane.
    d. They forget to turn their signal off.

8. Which is the defining characteristic of road rage?
    a. The intention to harm other drivers
    b. Driving with disregard for others' safety
    c. Failing to obey traffic laws
    d. Abruptly switching lanes

9. What is the number one tip recommended for drowsy drivers?
    a. Drink caffeine.
    b. Crack a window and let in some cool air.
    c. Get some sleep.
    d. Do some exercise before getting on the road.

10. Which description of fog is accurate?
    a. Solid precipitation from cumulonimbus clouds
    b. A thin, clear glaze of ice on roads and other surfaces
    c. Water droplets that appear on blades of grass and other thin objects
    d. A cloud that forms and hangs when water vapor doesn't completely dissipate

11. Which of the following is least likely to impair a driver?
    a. Wine
    b. Marijuana
    c. Barbiturates
    d. Caffeine

12. What does BAC stand for?
    a. Blood alcohol content
    b. Blood alcohol concentration
    c. Body alcohol concentration
    d. Body alcohol calculation

13. Which of the following is considered a hazardous material?
    a. Fireworks
    b. Water
    c. Rubber
    d. Plastic

14. What does antifreeze do?
    a. It keeps the windows from icing in wintry weather.
    b. It protects the engine from overheating or freezing.
    c. It is mixed in with gasoline to extend the vehicle's mileage.
    d. It is used to wash the windshield.

15. What do winterfronts do?
    a. They protect the windshield from ice.
    b. They cover and protect the grille.
    c. They protect the tires from losing tread.
    d. They help the truck warm up faster.

Practice Test

16. How often should a driver stop to check tire pressure when driving in hot weather?
    a. Every 200 miles
    b. Every 50 miles
    c. Every 150 miles
    d. Every 100 miles

17. What is a level crossing?
    a. Standard railroad tracks
    b. A subway line
    c. The intersection of a railroad and a highway
    d. A pedestrian crosswalk

18. What is an escape ramp?
    a. An off-road lane for trucks experiencing emergencies
    b. The "shoulder" area outside of a lane
    c. The first exit off a highway
    d. A bridge over a roadway

19. What do anti-lock brakes do?
    a. They help the regular brakes function.
    b. They keep the wheels from locking.
    c. They keep the brakes from locking.
    d. They bring the vehicle to a stop.

20. What is skidding?
    a. When tires blow out
    b. When tires lose traction on the road
    c. When the vehicle tilts to the side
    d. When the vehicle's brakes fail

21. Why is it important for the driver to take pictures at the scene of an accident they are involved in?
    a. The police may ask the driver for them.
    b. They will help emergency respondents understand what happened.
    c. The driver can upload them to social media.
    d. The driver's insurer may need visual evidence of the incident.

22. Which of the following is a type of fire extinguisher?
    a. ABC
    b. BS
    c. ABS
    d. CD

23. How are hazard placards typically shaped?
    a. Square
    b. Triangle
    c. Diamond
    d. Octagon

Practice Test

24. If a driver commits three traffic violations in a CMV within three years, what is the minimum amount of time their CDL could be suspended?
    a. 60 days
    b. 120 days
    c. 30 days
    d. 1 year

25. Which of the following is a qualification for the International Registration Plan (IRP) certification?
    a. The vehicle has two axles and weighs more than 26,000 pounds.
    b. The vehicle has one axle and air brakes.
    c. The vehicle has an anti-lock brake system.
    d. The vehicle is registered under the International Fuel Tax Agreement (IFTA).

26. What does GVWR stand for?
    a. Gravitational vehicle weight requirements
    b. Gross vehicle weight rating
    c. Gravitational vehicle weight rating
    d. Gross vehicle weight requirements

27. Which of the following is NOT an example of an item that would be used to secure cargo?
    a. Covers
    b. Header boards
    c. Bricks
    d. Tie-downs

28. Coffee, grains, raw minerals, and metals are examples of which of the following?
    a. Dry bulk
    b. Breakbulk
    c. Roll-on/roll-off cargo
    d. Liquid bulk

29. Which of the following is NOT an example of a hazardous material?
    a. Fuel
    b. Corrosives
    c. Grains
    d. Laundry detergent

30. What is the minimum distance a bus driver should stop from a railroad crossing before proceeding?
    a. 10 feet
    b. 15 feet
    c. 50 feet
    d. 5 feet

31. How should a driver handle a disruptive passenger?
    a. Immediately call the police.
    b. Physically remove the passenger from the vehicle.
    c. Stay calm and let the passenger stay for the remainder of the trip.
    d. Stop at a safe location and ask the passenger to get out.

32. When should drivers fuel or refuel their vehicles?
    a. When passengers are not on board
    b. Every 15 miles
    c. When they are completely out of fuel
    d. After they reach their destination

33. When are a vehicle's brake-door interlocks activated?
    a. When the brakes are tapped
    b. When the emergency brake is used
    c. When a vehicle's rear door opens while its throttle is idle
    d. When the front door opens while the throttle is idle

34. How should most flanks of meat be transported?
    a. On dry ice in the back of a trailer
    b. Hanging in a refrigerated truck
    c. Salted and packaged in Styrofoam coolers
    d. Wrapped in plastic in a refrigerated truck

35. Which step of the air brake testing process is testing the governor cut-out?
    a. First
    b. Fourth
    c. Seventh
    d. Third

36. On which type of vehicles are dual air brakes usually installed?
    a. Heavy-duty vehicles
    b. Minivans
    c. Passenger cars
    d. Pickup trucks

37. What is the calculation for stopping distance?
    a. *Perception distance + braking distance + brake lag*
    b. *Reaction distance + perception distance + braking distance + brake lag*
    c. *Reaction distance + braking distance + brake lag*
    d. *Braking distance + perception distance + reaction distance*

38. What does an alcohol evaporator do?
    a. Removes alcohol from inside the storage tank
    b. Drains the storage tank
    c. Pumps alcohol into the storage tank to prevent ice
    d. Pumps out of the storage tank

39. Which statement about the trailer air supply control is true?
    a. It controls the flow of air to the tractor.
    b. Its knob automatically pushes in when the tractor protection valve closes.
    c. It protects the tractor brakes if there's an air pressure loss.
    d. It sends airflow to turn the trailer's emergency brakes on.

Practice Test

40. What does the service line do?
    a. It connects to the red glad hand on the trailer.
    b. It controls the service brakes.
    c. It controls the trailer's emergency brake.
    d. It fills the trailer air tanks with air.

41. On a combination vehicle, when should shut-off valves be open, and on which trailers?
    a. On all trailers, before driving when multiple trailers are connected
    b. On all trailers, except the last one when multiple trailers are connected
    c. On a single trailer, when no additional trailers are connected
    d. On any trailer, when the emergency line is connected

42. Which of the following trailers would definitely have antilock brakes (ABS)?
    a. A trailer built in 1985
    b. A trailer with a yellow light on the left front or rear corner
    c. A trailer with ECU and sensor wires coming from the brakes
    d. Both b and c

43. If the trailer is too high when coupling, what may happen?
    a. The air lines may not reach the trailer.
    b. The kingpin may be too low for the fifth wheel.
    c. The tractor and trailer may not couple correctly.
    d. The trailer nose may get damaged.

44. When properly coupled, how far apart should the upper and lower fifth wheel be?
    a. They should be as far apart as the length of the kingpin.
    b. They should be at least six inches apart.
    c. They should be far enough apart to see between them.
    d. They should be touching with no visible space between them.

45. How do you know if the kingpin is locked into the fifth wheel?
    a. You see the locking jaws on the kingpin head when looking into the back of the fifth wheel.
    b. You see the locking jaws on the kingpin head when looking into the front of the fifth wheel.
    c. You see the locking jaws on the kingpin shank when looking into the back of the fifth wheel.
    d. You see the locking jaws on the kingpin shank when looking into the front of the fifth wheel.

46. After coupling and before driving, where should the landing gear be?
    a. At least one foot off the ground
    b. Fully raised
    c. Just off the ground
    d. On the ground

47. How can you be sure that air is flowing to all trailers in a combination vehicle when there is air in the emergency and service lines?
    a. Air is coming from both air lines at the rear of the last trailer when shut-off valves are opened.
    b. No air is coming from either air line at the rear of the last trailer when shut-off valves are opened.
    c. The trailer air supply knob is out.
    d. All the vehicle's shut-off valves are closed.

Practice Test

48. How do you know the trailer emergency brakes are working?
   a. The trailer does not move easily when the air supply knob is pushed in.
   b. The trailer does not move easily when the air supply valve is turned to "normal."
   c. The trailer moves easily when the air supply knob is pushed in.
   d. The trailer moves easily when the air supply valve is turned to "emergency."

49. What does a yellow light on the left side of a converter dolly mean?
   a. It can couple a third trailer.
   b. It has antilock brakes (ABS).
   c. It has hazard lights.
   d. It has two axles.

50. Which of the following is the correct order for uncoupling a triple trailer?
   a. Uncouple the first trailer, unhitch the middle dolly and uncouple the second trailer, unhitch the rear dolly, and then uncouple the third trailer.
   b. Unhitch the middle dolly and uncouple the second trailer, unhitch the rear dolly and uncouple the third trailer, and then uncouple front trailer.
   c. Uncouple the second trailer and unhitch the middle dolly, uncouple the third trailer and unhitch the rear dolly, and then uncouple front trailer.
   d. Uncouple the third trailer and unhitch the rear dolly, uncouple the second trailer and unhitch the middle dolly, and then uncouple front trailer.

51. Which of the following describes the correct set up of the shut-off valves in the double and triple combination vehicles?
   a. All valves should be closed.
   b. All valves should be open.
   c. Only the valves on the rearmost trailer or dolly should be closed.
   d. Only the valves on the rearmost trailer or dolly should be open.

52. If you hear air when you open the air line shut-off valves on rearmost trailer, what is true?
   a. The brakes are malfunctioning.
   b. The brakes are working.
   c. The tractor protection valve isn't working.
   d. There is a leak in the air line.

53. How do you test the trailer service brakes after coupling?
   a. Apply the parking brake and use the trailer hand valve to engage the brakes.
   b. Press the foot brake to release air from the system and engage the tractor protection valve.
   c. Pull the air supply knob to engage the emergency brakes.
   d. Release the parking brake and use the trailer hand valve to engage the brakes.

54. Which type of tank is most likely to carry liquid food products?
   a. Baffled tank
   b. Bulkhead tank
   c. Smoothbore tank
   d. Any of them might be used to carry liquid food products

Practice Test

55. Which of the following situations makes it unsafe to drive a tank vehicle?
    a. The manhole covers are open.
    b. There are no signs of leaks.
    c. The valves are closed.
    d. The vents are clear and working properly.

56. What is outage in a tank vehicle?
    a. A bulkhead left empty to balance weight
    b. Movement of liquid in the tank during stops
    c. Overflow from the tank manhole
    d. Space left in the tank for liquid expansion

57. Which of the following is a safe driving rule for tank vehicles?
    a. Change lanes quickly to reduce surge in the tank.
    b. Hold the brake longer than usual after applying it at a stop.
    c. Leave less stopping distance than you would in traditional tractor-trailers.
    d. Take curves while driving at least the posted speed limit.

58. When is a surge most likely to affect vehicle handling?
    a. When accelerating quickly
    b. When braking steadily
    c. When driving smoothly
    d. When looking ahead while driving

59. Flammable gases are part of which hazard class?
    a. Class 2
    b. Class 4
    c. Class 6
    d. Class 9

60. Which hazard class is battery fluid a part of?
    a. Class 1
    b. Class 3
    c. Class 7
    d. Class 8

61. How many digits do hazardous material ID numbers usually have?
    a. Four
    b. Five
    c. Six
    d. Seven

62. How many columns does the hazardous materials table have?
    a. 10
    b. 11
    c. 12
    d. 13

Practice Test

63. Which of the following is not the name of a column in the hazardous materials table?
    a. Symbols
    b. Hazard class
    c. Identification numbers
    d. GP

64. What does the "D" symbol mean on the hazardous materials table?
    a. Domestic trading
    b. Domestic transportation
    c. Delayed transportation
    d. Delayed trading

65. What does "PG" stand for on the hazardous materials table?
    a. Packaged garments
    b. Packaging group
    c. Parts group
    d. Particulates group

66. To which agency should you report the spill of a hazardous substance?
    a. Department of Energy
    b. Defense Health Agency
    c. Environmental Protection Agency
    d. Federal Emergency Management Agency

67. Where should the shipper's certification be displayed?
    a. Warning placards
    b. Shipping label
    c. On the CMV
    d. Shipping paperwork

68. What must you sign if you transport hazardous waste?
    a. Uniform hazardous waste manifest
    b. Nondisclosure agreement
    c. Health disclosure form
    d. Insurance contract

69. How far away from other markings and attachments should placards be placed?
    a. 1 inch
    b. 2 Inches
    c. 3 inches
    d. 4 inches

70. Which of the following is an example of an explosive?
    a. Fireworks
    b. Propane
    c. Gasoline
    d. Potassium cyanide

Practice Test

71. How far before each bus stop must bus drivers use their right turn signal?
    a. At least 50 feet
    b. At least 300 feet
    c. At least 200 feet
    d. At least 100 feet

72. When stopping at a bus stop, how much distance should bus drivers leave between the front of their bus and the spot where children stand?
    a. At least 20 feet
    b. No distance
    c. At least 10 feet
    d. At least 5 feet

73. During the loading process en route, what should bus drivers do immediately before using your flashing lights?
    a. Open the door.
    b. Ensure that traffic has come to a stop.
    c. Give the signal for students to cross.
    d. Apply the parking brake.

74. What should bus drivers do if a child is unaccounted for?
    a. Contact the authorities.
    b. Ask other students if they have seen the missing student.
    c. Check around the outside of the bus.
    d. B and C only

75. In the event of an evacuation, what distance from a school bus is considered a safe location, assuming that the bus is not stranded on a highway or railroad tracks and that no toxins are present?
    a. At least 300 feet
    b. At least 50 feet
    c. At least 100 feet
    d. At least 500 feet

76. Which situation does NOT require the evacuation of a school bus?
    a. When a student inside the bus has suffered a neck injury
    b. When there is an engine fire
    c. When the scent or sight of gasoline is present
    d. When a school bus is stalled near railroad tracks

77. Which sentence best describes what to do at railroad crossing sites with multiple tracks?
    a. Stop once at each track to check for danger.
    b. Stop once at the crossing site and then cross every track without stopping again.
    c. Call the dispatcher to find information about alternative routes.
    d. Put the bus in reverse and backtrack to a safer route.

78. What is the smallest acceptable distance for bus drivers to stop before railroad tracks?
    a. 15 feet
    b. 10 feet
    c. 20 feet
    d. 25 feet

Practice Test

79. What is the longest acceptable distance for bus drivers to stop before railroad tracks?
    a. 25 feet
    b. 40 feet
    c. 75 feet
    d. 50 feet

80. What should bus drivers do when a student misbehaves during the loading or unloading process?
    a. Stop students from entering or exiting the bus and deal with unruly students immediately.
    b. Instruct unruly students to exit the bus.
    c. Complete loading or unloading procedures and deal with unruly students afterward.
    d. Deal with both unruly students and students entering or exiting the bus simultaneously.

81. When should bus drivers use their roof-mounted strobe lights?
    a. Only when visibility is severely impaired
    b. When visibility is impaired, either slightly or severely
    c. When crossing railroad tracks
    d. When encountering mechanical issues

82. When should bus drivers put their buses in reverse?
    a. When creating space between vehicles in traffic
    b. Only when no other option is available
    c. When creating space at railroad crossing sites
    d. After unloading students on streets with no other outlet

83. Which component is NOT part of a vehicle's suspension system?
    a. Suspension system indicator
    b. Coil springs
    c. Torque arms
    d. Torsion bars

84. Where on the vehicle do drivers ensure that mounts are stable?
    a. Where mounts are secured to the trailer's frame and axles
    b. Where mounts secure a powered and an unpowered vehicle
    c. Where mounts are secured to the tractor's frame and axles
    d. Everywhere that mounts are secured to the frame and axles

85. For vehicles with manual transmission, drivers should not be able to pull the brake pushrod more than which distance when the brakes are released?
    a. 1 foot
    b. 1 inch
    c. 2 feet
    d. 2 inches

86. What is the minimum acceptable tread depth for tires on the steering axle?
    a. 8/32
    b. 2/32
    c. 4/32
    d. 1/32

Practice Test

87. How many versions of the Class A Vehicle Inspection Test are there?
    a. 4
    b. 3
    c. 5
    d. 6

88. When do drivers find out which version of the Vehicle Inspection Test they will take?
    a. When the test is underway
    b. One week before the date of the test
    c. Immediately before the test begins
    d. Two days before the test

89. Which step is NOT part of the Class A Vehicle Inspection Test?
    a. Inspection of a distinct feature of a driver's particular vehicle
    b. In-cab inspection
    c. Inspection of the vehicle's coupling system
    d. Engine start

90. How many versions of the Class B and C Vehicle Inspection Test are there?
    a. 4
    b. 3
    c. 5
    d. 6

91. Which step is NOT part of the Class B and C Vehicle Inspection Test?
    a. Inspection of a distinct feature of a driver's particular vehicle
    b. In-cab inspection
    c. Inspection of the vehicle's coupling system
    d. Engine start

92. What is the minimum acceptable tread depth for tires everywhere except the steering axle?
    a. 8/32
    b. 2/32
    c. 4/32
    d. 1/32

93. Which exercises do drivers perform on both sides of their vehicle?
    a. Offset Backing and Straight-Line Backing
    b. Offset Backing and Parallel Parking
    c. Parallel Parking and Alley Docking
    d. Alley Docking and Offset Backing

94. When are drivers penalized for pull-ups?
    a. The second time they do a pull-up
    b. Never
    c. After the examiner decides they have done too many
    d. The first time the drive does a pull-up

95. When are drivers penalized for encroachments?
    a. After five in a row
    b. Never
    c. When the examiner decides the driver has done too many
    d. Each time

96. For Parallel Parking and Alley Docking exercises, how many looks are drivers permitted?
    a. One
    b. Two
    c. Four
    d. Five

97. For the Straight-Line Backing exercise, how many looks are drivers permitted?
    a. One
    b. Two
    c. Three
    d. None

98. Which of the following steps do drivers NOT take when completing a look?
    a. Put the vehicle in neutral and apply the parking brake
    b. Maintain three points of contact with the vehicle while exiting the vehicle
    c. Re-enter the vehicle once to ensure safety before proceeding
    d. Maintain a firm grip on handrails during dismount

99. How far from the back do drivers stop the vehicle when completing an Alley Dock exercise?
    a. Two feet
    b. Eight feet
    c. Five feet
    d. Three feet

100. When is an Offset Backing exercise complete?
    a. After the front of the vehicle clears the first set of cones
    b. When the driver steers the vehicle into the opposite lane
    c. After the driver moves the vehicle out of the way of traffic
    d. When the driver parks the vehicle three feet from the last set of cones

Answer Explanations

1. A: Drivers should always try to park in spots that they can easily pull through. Choices *B, C,* and *D* are not only incorrect but also potentially dangerous.

2. D: Choice *D* is correct because drivers should always check their mirrors and make sure nothing is behind them before backing up. Choice *A* is incorrect because, of the choices provided, it is the third step the driver would take. Choice *B* is incorrect because asking someone to guide you is usually a final step. Choice *C* is incorrect because checking the cargo should be done before entering the truck.

3. C: The last step for shifting to a higher gear involves pushing the accelerator and letting go of the clutch. Choices *A, B,* and *D* are incorrect because they are all precursors to the last step.

4. B: Choice *B* is correct; you should find a safe place to pull over and wait for the fog to dissipate. Choice *A* is incorrect because you should only keep driving and turn on the low beams when it is impossible to pull over. Choice *C* is incorrect because you should never turn on the high beams and speed through the fog. Choice *D* is incorrect because turning around in fog should only be done when necessary.

5. D: Choice *D* is correct; the driver should leave one second of space for every 10 feet of vehicle length.

6. A: Choice *A* is correct; calculating stopping distance usually isn't a distraction. Choices *B, C,* and *D* are all incorrect because talking over the dispatcher, adjusting mirrors, and having a bad temperament are all potential distractions while driving.

7. C: A driver weaving in and out of a traffic lane could be under the influence or falling asleep. Choices *A, B,* and *D* are incorrect; flashing high beams, talking on a cell phone, and forgetting to turn a signal off do not necessarily indicate that a driver is impaired.

8. A: Drivers with road rage intend to harm other drivers. Choice *B* is incorrect because it also describes the act of careless driving. While they describe actions that people with road rage might do, Choices *B, C,* and *D* do not completely describe road rage.

9. C: The first thing drowsy drivers are told to do is find a safe place to get some sleep. Choices *A, B,* and *D* are all helpful tips for combating drowsiness, but they are incorrect because they are not the first priority.

10. D: Fog is a cloud that forms and hangs when water vapor doesn't completely dissipate. Choice *A* is incorrect; solid precipitation from cumulonimbus clouds is hail. Choice *B* is incorrect; a thin, clear glaze of ice on roads and other surfaces is black ice. Choice *C* is incorrect because water droplets that appear on thin objects like blades of grass are dew.

11. D: While caffeine may have some side effects, it is less likely to impair a driver when compared to the other substances listed. Choices *A* and *B* are incorrect because alcohol and marijuana are known to impair drivers. Choice *C* is incorrect because barbiturates are incredibly dangerous when taken before driving.

12. B: Choice *B* is correct because BAC stands for blood alcohol concentration.

13. A: Fireworks are hazardous materials. Choices *B, C,* and *D* are incorrect because water, rubber, and plastic are not hazardous materials.

Answer Explanations

14. B: Antifreeze protects the engine from overheating and freezing. Choice *A* is incorrect because antifreeze does not keep the windows from icing. Choice *C* is incorrect because antifreeze should not be mixed with gasoline. Choice *D* is incorrect because antifreeze is not the same as washer fluid, which is used to clean windshields.

15. B: Winterfronts cover truck grilles and protect them from winter weather. Choices *A*, *C*, and *D* are incorrect because winterfronts don't protect windshields or tires, and they don't help vehicles warm up faster.

16. D: When it is hot outside, a driver should check the tire pressure every 100 miles.

17. C: A level crossing is where a railroad and a highway intersect.

18. A: Escape ramps enable trucks to pull off the highway during emergencies.

19. B: Antilock brakes keep the wheels from locking up after braking too hard. Choice *A* is incorrect because antilock brakes have nothing to do with regular brakes and do not help them function. Choice *C* is incorrect because antilock brakes don't keep the brakes from locking. Finally, Choice *D* is incorrect because these brakes do not make the vehicle stop.

20. B: Skidding happens when tires lose traction on the road.

21. D: Choice *D* is correct; the insurer may want pictures of the damage caused by the accident. Choice *A* is incorrect because the police are unlikely to ask the driver for photos of the scene. Choice *B* is incorrect because emergency respondents are unlikely to use the photos to figure out what happened. Choice *C* is incorrect because it is not helpful, and is possibly a violation of privacy, to upload photos of the accident to social media.

22. A: ABC is a type of fire extinguisher that puts out fires on cloth, paper, wood, or other fabrics. The other choices are not types of fire extinguishers.

23. C: Hazard placards are usually diamond shaped.

24. B: Committing three traffic violations in a CMV within three years can result in a 120-day CDL suspension.

25. A: A two-axle vehicle weighing more than 26,000 pounds is one of the two qualifications for the IRP certification. Choices *B*, *C*, and *D* are incorrect; having one axle and air brakes, having an anti-lock brake system, and being registered under the IFTA are not qualifications for the IRP certification.

26. B: GVWR stands for gross vehicle weight rating.

27. C: Bricks are not used to secure cargo. Choices *A*, *B*, and *D* are incorrect because covers, header boards, and tie-downs are used to secure cargo.

28. A: Coffee, grains, raw minerals, and metals are types of dry bulk cargo. Choice *B* is incorrect; breakbulk cargo usually includes items such as wind turbines, wood, and paper. Choice *C* is incorrect because roll-on/roll-off cargo includes cars, trucks, cranes, and other vehicles. Choice *D* is incorrect; oil and fuel are types of liquid bulk.

29. C: Grain is not a hazardous material. Fuel, corrosives, and laundry detergent are hazardous materials.

Answer Explanations

30. B: A driver should stop a minimum of 15 feet from a rail crossing. Choices *A* and *D* are incorrect because 5-10 feet is not far enough away. Choice *C* is incorrect because 50 feet is the *maximum* distance a driver should stop from a rail crossing.

31. D: Wait until it's safe and then ask the passenger to get out. Choice *A* is incorrect because not all disruptive behavior requires police assistance. Choice *B* is incorrect; the driver should never physically remove a passenger. Choice *C* is incorrect because a disruptive passenger should not be allowed to remain in the vehicle for the duration of the trip since they could endanger other passengers.

32. A: It is safest to fuel or refuel when passengers are not on board. Choice *B* is incorrect because fueling up every 15 miles would be unnecessary and inefficient. Choice *C* is incorrect; it is unwise to wait until the tank is completely empty to fuel up. Choice *D* is incorrect because the driver will likely run out of fuel before reaching the destination.

33. C: Brake-door interlocks activate when a vehicle's rear door opens while its throttle is idle. Choices *A*, *B*, and *D* are incorrect because they do not activate in any of the other described scenarios.

34. B: Flanks of meat should be transported hanging in a refrigerated truck. The remaining choices are incorrect because they describe improper ways to transport meat.

35. D: Testing the governor cut-out is the third step. Choice *A* is incorrect because the first step is testing the low-air warning device. Choice *B* is incorrect because the fourth step is testing the governor cut-in. Choice *C* is incorrect because the seventh step is testing the spring brakes.

36. A: Dual air brakes are usually installed on heavy-duty vehicles. Choices *B*, *C*, and *D* are incorrect; they are all light-duty vehicles and do not use dual air brakes.

37. B: The calculation for stopping distance is *reaction distance* + *perception distance* + *braking distance* + *brake lag*. The remaining choices are missing one element of the equation.

38. C: An alcohol evaporator pumps alcohol into the storage tank to prevent ice. The remaining choices do not describe the function of an alcohol evaporator.

39. C: Choice *C* is correct because the trailer air supply control closes the tractor protection valve if the pressure in the system falls to between 20 and 45 psi due to an air leak. This maintains air in the tractor brake system so that it can continue to function if there is a leak in the trailer line or the trailer becomes separated from the tractor. Choice *A* is incorrect because the trailer supply control deals with air in the trailer, not the tractor. Choice *B* is incorrect because the trailer air supply control knob automatically pops out when the tractor protection valve closes at low pressures. When the knob is pushed in, the tractor protection valve opens. Choice *D* is incorrect because the trailer's emergency brakes turn on when air pressure drops. When air is flowing through the emergency line, the emergency brakes are kept off the trailer wheels.

40. B: Choice *B* is correct because the service line sends an air signal to the relay valve, which sends a corresponding amount of air pressure to the service brakes, which are the brakes that stop the vehicle while moving. Choice *A* is incorrect because the service line and associated parts are usually colored blue; the emergency line and associated parts are colored red. Choice *C* is incorrect because the emergency line controls the trailer's emergency brake; it keeps the emergency brake off the wheels when the system is pressurized. The trailer's emergency brake engages when there is a loss of pressure in the emergency line. Choice *D* is incorrect because the emergency line fills the trailer air tanks with air. The service line only

Answer Explanations

sends a signal to the relay valve to engage the service brakes when the foot pedal or hand brake are applied.

41. B: Choice *B* is correct because valves are open on combination vehicles to allow air flow to all the connected dollies and trailers. The valves on the last trailer should be closed. Choice *A* is incorrect because the last trailer in a combination vehicle should have its valves closed to prevent air loss from the system. Choice *C* is incorrect because the single trailer with no other trailers connected should have its valves closed to prevent air loss. Choice *D* is incorrect because all trailers should have an emergency line connected, but the last trailer in the combination vehicle should have its shut-off valves closed.

42. D: Choice *D* is correct because Choices *B* and *C* are both correct. Trailers built after March 1, 1988, must have ABS and have a yellow ABS light in either the front or rear corner. Trailers built before that date may not have a yellow ABS light, but they will have ECU and sensor wires coming from the brakes if they have been retrofitted with ABS. Choice *A* is incorrect because trailers built before March 1, 1988, were not required to have ABS. Though they may be retrofitted with ABS, it is possible they have not. Choices *B* and *C* are individually true, but Choice *D* is the best answer because it encapsulates both correct answer choices.

43. C: Choice *C* is correct because if the trailer is too high, the kingpin will not fit in the locking jaws of the fifth wheel skid plate, and they will not fit together. Choice *A* is incorrect because the height of the trailer should not affect the ability of the air lines to reach it when the tractor is close enough. Choice *B* is incorrect because the kingpin would only be too low for the fifth wheel if the trailer were too low while coupling. If the trailer were too low, the tractor would likely hit the trailer nose before it could be backed far enough to reach the kingpin. Choice *D* is incorrect because the trailer nose is likely to get damaged if the trailer is too low when coupling and the tractor hits the trailer nose.

44. D: Choice *D* is correct because the upper and lower fifth wheel should be touching with no visible space between them when properly coupled. Choice *A* is incorrect because if they were a kingpin's length apart, the kingpin would not be able to lock into the skid plate of the lower fifth wheel. Choice *B* is incorrect because if they are six inches apart, the locking jaws of the skid plate will not engage properly with the kingpin. Choice *C* is incorrect because there should be no visible space between the upper and lower fifth wheel to ensure proper coupling.

45. C: Choice *C* is correct because you should check the coupling by looking into the back of the fifth wheel, and when properly coupled, the locking jaws should be on the shank of the kingpin, not the head. Choice *A* is incorrect because the locking jaws should be on the kingpin shank, not the kingpin head when properly coupled. Choice *B* is incorrect because you should check the fit of the kingpin from the back of the fifth wheel; you will not be able to see it well from the front. Also, the locking jaws should be on the shank of the kingpin rather than the head. Choice *D* is incorrect because you should check the fit of the kingpin from the back of the fifth wheel; you will not be able to see it well from the front.

46. B: Choice *B* is correct because the landing gear should be fully raised with the crank safely secured before driving. This prevents the landing gear from hitting the tractor while turning or potentially hitting railroad crossings or other bumps in the road while driving. Choices *A*, *C*, and *D* are incorrect because the landing gear should be fully raised to avoid hitting anything when moving.

47. A: Choice *A* is correct because hearing air coming from the last trailer shows that it is flowing throughout the whole vehicle system to operate each vehicle's brakes. Choice *B* is incorrect because if there is no air escaping at the end of the last trailer, the air is being stopped somewhere along the way before getting to that trailer, and the brakes may not function correctly. Choice *C* is incorrect because the

Answer Explanations

trailer air supply knob should be pushed in to send air to the trailers, so you can make sure that it is flowing all the way to the last trailer in the system. Choice *D* is incorrect because only the shut-off valves on the last trailer in the system should be closed. Shut-off valves on other trailers should be open to allow air to pass to trailers behind them.

48. C: Choice *C* is correct because when the trailer air supply knob is pushed in, air is sent to the trailer, which takes the emergency brake off the trailer wheels and allows the trailer to move easily. Choice *A* is incorrect for the same reason; the trailer *does* move easily in this situation. Choice *B* is incorrect because when the air supply valve is turned to "normal," air is sent to the trailer, which takes the emergency brake off the trailer wheels and allows the trailer to move freely. Choice *D* is incorrect because when the air supply valve is turned to "emergency," air flow to the trailer is stopped, which engages the emergency brake that should keep the trailer from moving.

49. B: Choice *B* is correct because dollies built after March 1, 1988, have ABS and a yellow indicator on their left sides. Choice *A* is incorrect because the yellow light does not relate to coupling. Choice *C* is incorrect because the yellow light does not relate to other lights on the dolly. Choice *D* is incorrect because the yellow light does not relate to the number of axles on the dolly.

50. D: Choice *D* is correct because back to front is the correct order for uncoupling a triple trailer. Choice *A* is incorrect because if you uncouple the front trailer from the tractor first, you will not be able to use the tractor to move the trailers or the dollies. Choice *B* is incorrect because a dolly should always be uncoupled from the trailer behind it before being unhitched from the trailer in front of it. Choice *C* is incorrect because the vehicle should be uncoupled starting from the rear and moving forward.

51. C: Choice *C* is correct because the valves in the middle of the vehicle should be open to allow air to travel to the rear of the vehicle, but the valves on the end of the last trailer should be closed to prevent air loss from the system. Choice *A* is incorrect because if the valves in the middle of the vehicle are closed, there will be no air supply to brakes in any of the trailers or dollies behind them. Choice *B* is incorrect because if the valves on the rearmost trailer are open, the system will not be able to maintain pressure to operate the brakes. Choice *D* is incorrect because if the valves in the middle of the vehicle are closed, there will be no air supply to the brakes in any of the trailers or dollies behind them.

52. B: Choice *B* is correct because hearing air from open lines at the rearmost trailer indicates that the whole system is charged with air, and the brakes should be functional. Choice *A* is incorrect because if the brakes were not working, there would be no sound of air. Choice *C* is incorrect because the tractor protection valve doesn't engage to cut off air flow to the trailers automatically until the system pressure drops to between 20 and 45 psi, which indicates a large loss of air from the system. Choice *D* is incorrect because air should come through the lines when the shut-off valves are open. If air can be heard when the shut-off valves are closed on the rearmost trailer, there may be a leak.

53. D: Choice *D* is correct because the trailer hand valve only engages the trailer brakes; if it activates the brakes while the parking brake is off, the service brakes are working. Choice *A* is incorrect because with the parking brake on, you will not be able to tell if the trailer hand valve is engaging the service brakes. Choice *B* is incorrect because the tractor protection valve engages when there is not enough air in the system to operate the trailer service brakes. Choice *C* is incorrect because the emergency brakes engage when there is not enough air in the system to operate the trailer service brakes.

54. C: Choice *C* is correct because smoothbore tanks, having no separators, are the easiest to sanitize and thus the best for food. Choices *A*, *B*, and *D* are incorrect because baffled tanks and bulkheads are more difficult to sanitize.

Answer Explanations

55. A: Choice *A* is correct because manholes should always be covered before operating a tank vehicle. Choice *B* is incorrect because, for safe operation, there should be no signs of leaks. Choice *C* is incorrect because all valves should be closed for safe operation. Choice *D* is incorrect because vents should be clear and working properly for safe operation.

56. D: Choice *D* is correct because outage is the space left in a tank to allow for the expansion of liquid when it heats up during transport. Choice *A* is incorrect because outage is not related to weight balancing. Choice *B* is incorrect because the movement of liquid in the tank is called a surge. Choice *C* is incorrect because outage is space in the tank to prevent an overflow.

57. B: Choice *B* is correct; to reduce the possibility that a surge will push the truck forward after braking, you should hold the brake for an extended period of time in a tank vehicle. Choice *A* is incorrect because changing lanes quickly will increase the side-to-side surge in a tank vehicle. Choice *C* is incorrect because you should leave a greater stopping distance in tank trucks to allow slow, smooth braking. Choice *D* is incorrect because you should take curves at below the posted speed limit in tank vehicles to reduce the risk of rollover.

58. A: Choice *A* is correct because accelerating quickly will cause the liquid in the tank to move toward the back of the tank and pull the vehicle backward. Choice *B* is incorrect because smooth, steady braking will help to slow the movement of liquid in the tank and reduce surge. Choice *C* is incorrect because smooth driving reduces surge and should improve vehicle handling. Choice *D* is incorrect because looking ahead while driving should limit the need for fast stops or abrupt turns, reducing the risk of surge.

59. B: Flammable gases are part of Class 4 hazardous materials.

60. D: Battery fluid is a Class 8 hazardous material.

61. A: Hazardous material ID numbers usually have four digits.

62. A: The hazardous materials table has 10 columns.

63. D: "GP" is not the name of a column in the hazardous materials table. Choices *A*, *B*, and *C* are incorrect; "symbols," "hazard class," and "identification numbers" are hazmat table column names.

64. B: "D" stands for "domestic transportation."

65. B: "PG" stands for "packaging group."

66. C: You should report hazardous substance spills to the Environmental Protection Agency.

67. D: The shipper's certification should be on the shipping paperwork.

68. A: If you transport hazardous waste, you must sign a uniform hazardous waste manifest. Choices *B*, *C*, and *D* are incorrect; you do not need to sign a nondisclosure agreement, health disclosure form, or insurance contract.

69. C: Placards should be placed three inches away from other markings or attachments.

70. A: Choice *A* is correct because fireworks are types of explosives. Choice *B* is incorrect; propane is a flammable gas. Choice *C* is incorrect because gasoline is a flammable liquid. Choice *D* is incorrect; potassium cyanide is a type of poison.

Answer Explanations

71. D: Choice *D* is correct because bus drivers must use their right turn signal at least 100 feet before each bus stop.

72. C: Bus drivers must leave at least 10 feet of space between the front of the bus and where children wait. This precaution helps prevent accidents. Choice *A* is incorrect because bus drivers are not compelled to leave a distance of at least 20 feet between the front of their buses and the spot where children wait. Choices *B* and *D* are incorrect because it is unsafe to leave less than 10 feet of distance.

73. B: Choice *B* is correct because the bus's flashing lights are one of the signs children look for before they approach the bus. Drivers should not give children any signal to approach until they are certain that all oncoming traffic has come to a stop. Choice *A* is incorrect because school bus drivers open the doors only after they turn on their flashing lights. Choice *C* is incorrect because bus drivers should not give children the signal to cross until after they turn on their flashing lights. Choice *D* is incorrect because bus drivers use their parking brake when they put their buses in neutral and come to a stop.

74. D: Choice *D* is the correct answer because bus drivers should do both things listed in Choices *B* and *C*. They should ask other children to confirm the whereabouts of the missing child, and they should check outside the bus to ensure that a student is not trapped or hiding. Choice *A* is incorrect because bus drivers don't need to contact authorities about absent students.

75. C: Students should find a safe location at least 100 feet from the school bus during an evacuation. Choice *A* is incorrect because students only need to move 300 feet from the school bus when they are evacuated because of toxins or because the bus is stuck on a highway or railroad tracks. Choice *B* is incorrect because it does not meet the minimum distance required for children to evacuate to during a standard emergency. Choice *D* is incorrect because it exceeds the distance required for children to evacuate to during a standard emergency.

76. A: Choice *A* is correct because a child who suffers a neck injury should not be moved for fear of worsening the injury, and the remaining passengers need not be evacuated either. The remaining choices are incorrect because an evacuation must occur when fire is present, if there is a gasoline leak, or when a bus is stalled on or near railroad tracks.

77. B: Choice *B* is correct because bus drivers stop once in front of the crossing site before crossing all tracks without stopping. It is very dangerous to stop on railroad tracks, and bus drivers should follow correct protocol to traverse multiple railroad tracks efficiently. Choice *A* is incorrect because bus drivers should never stop after they have begun to cross a set of railroad tracks. Choice *C* is incorrect because it is unnecessary for bus drivers to seek alternative routes when they encounter a railroad crossing site with multiple railroad tracks. Choice *D* is incorrect because bus drivers should put their buses in reverse only when they have no safer option available.

78. A: Bus drivers must never stop their buses closer than 15 feet to railroad tracks. In most cases, a white line appears on the road before railroad tracks to mark this distance, but drivers can also refer to the railroad crossing traffic sign when a white line is absent. Choice *B* is incorrect because bus drivers should never stop within 15 feet of a railroad track. Choices *C* and *D* are incorrect because, while both answer choices indicate acceptable distances for drivers to stop their buses before railroad tracks, neither indicates the smallest acceptable distance.

79. D: Choice *D* is correct because 50 feet is the longest distance that bus drivers should leave between their buses and railroad tracks. Choices *A* and *B* are incorrect because, while both answer choices indicate

Answer Explanations

acceptable distances for bus drivers to stop their buses before railroad tracks, neither is the longest acceptable distance. Choice *C* is incorrect because it exceeds the maximum distance.

80. C: Choice *C* is correct because bus drivers must give students entering or exiting the school bus their full attention. Accidents happen when drivers are distracted. Choice *A* is incorrect because bus drivers must prioritize loading and unloading procedures. Choice *B* is incorrect because bus drivers should never let students out at any location other than at school or their scheduled drop-off point. Choice *D* is incorrect because bus drivers must put their full attention on students as they enter or exit the bus.

81. B: Bus drivers should use their strobe lights when visibility is either slightly or severely impaired because they help buses stand out on the road. Choice *A* is incorrect because bus drivers should use their strobe lights whenever visibility is affected, not just during severe impairment. Choice *C* is incorrect because bus drivers use their caution lights when approaching railroad tracks, rather than their strobe light. Choice *D* is incorrect because bus drivers do not use their strobe lights to indicate mechanical issues.

82. B: Choice *B* is correct because driving school buses in reverse is extremely dangerous; therefore, drivers should put their buses in reverse only when there is no other option. Choice *A* is incorrect because bus drivers should always leave space between their bus and other vehicles in traffic, without needing to back up. Choice *C* is incorrect because bus drivers must stop at least 15 feet between the front of their bus and railroad tracks; they should not drive closer and then back up to 15 feet. Choice *D* is incorrect because school bus drivers must never back up when students are outside the bus. School bus routes are set so that drivers never travel down streets that have no other outlet.

83. A: Choice *A* is correct because suspension systems do not have a suspension system indicator. Choices *B*, *C*, and *D* are incorrect because coil springs, torque arms, and torsion bars are integral parts of a vehicle's suspension system, and drivers must ensure that they are present and in working order.

84. D: Choice *D* is correct because drivers ensure the integrity and stability of mounts everywhere that mounts are secured to the frame and axles. Choices *A* and *C* are incorrect because drivers do not only ensure the integrity and stability of mounts on certain parts of the vehicle. Choice *B* is incorrect because mounts are not used to secure two vehicles together.

85. B: Choice *B* is correct because drivers should not be able to pull the brake pushrod more than one inch from its resting position while the brakes are released. Choices *A*, *C*, and *D* are incorrect because all these distances are greater than one inch.

86. C: Choice *C* is correct because 4/32 is the minimum acceptable tread depth for tires on the steering axle. Choice *A* is incorrect because 8/32 exceeds the minimum. Choice *B* is incorrect because 2/32 is the minimum acceptable tread depth for tires everywhere other than on the steering axle. Choice *D* is incorrect because 1/32 is smaller than the minimum acceptable tread depth for tires on the steering axle.

87. A: There are four versions of the Class A Vehicle Inspection Test.

88. C: Choice *C* is correct because drivers find out which version of the Vehicle Inspection Test they will take immediately before the test begins.

89. A: Choice *A* is correct because inspection of a distinct feature of a driver's particular vehicle is part of the Class B and C Vehicle Inspection Test, not the Class A Vehicle Inspection Test. Choices *B*, *C*, and *D* are incorrect because these are part of the Class A Vehicle Inspection Test.

90. B: There are three versions of the Class B and C Vehicle Inspection Test.

Answer Explanations

91. C: Choice *C* is correct because inspection of the vehicle's coupling system is part of the Class A Vehicle Inspection Test, not the Class B and C Vehicle Inspection Test. Choices *A*, *B*, and *D* are incorrect because these are steps in the Class B and C Vehicle Inspection Test.

92. B: Choice *B* is correct because 2/32 is the minimum acceptable tread depth for tires everywhere except the steering axle. Choice *A* is incorrect because 8/32 exceeds this minimum. Choice *C* is incorrect because 4/32 is the minimum acceptable tread depth for tires on the steering axle only. Choice *D* is incorrect because 1/32 is smaller than the minimum acceptable tread depth for tires everywhere except the steering axle.

93. B: Choice *B* is correct because drivers may complete Offset Backing and Parallel Parking exercises on both sides of the vehicle. Choice *A* is incorrect because drivers complete Straight Line Backing exercises in only one direction. Choice *C* is incorrect because drivers complete Alley Docking exercises in only one direction. Choice *D* is incorrect because, while drivers may complete Offset Backing exercises on either side of the vehicle, drivers complete Alley Docking exercises only at the back of the vehicle.

94. C: Choice *C* is correct because drivers are penalized for doing an excessive number of pull-ups, rather than a set number of pull-ups. Choices *A* and *D* are incorrect because drivers are not penalized for a small number of pull-ups. Choice *B* is incorrect because drivers are penalized for pull-ups after they do too many.

95. D: Drivers are penalized for each encroachment.

96. B: Choice *B* is correct because drivers are allowed two looks for most exercises. This Includes Alley Docking and Parallel Parking exercises. Choice *A* is incorrect because drivers are permitted only one look for some exercises. For example, drivers are permitted only one look for the Straight-Line Backing exercise. Choices *C* and *D* are incorrect because neither number indicates the number of looks allocated to drivers for driving exercises.

97. A: Choice *A* is correct because drivers are allowed only one look for the Straight-Line Backing exercise. Choice *B* is incorrect because, while drivers are allowed two looks for most exercises, they are allowed only one look for the Straight-Line Backing exercise. Choices *C* and *D* are incorrect because only one look is permitted for the Straight-Line Backing exercise.

98. C: Choice *C* is correct because this is not one of the steps drivers take when completing a look. Choice *A* is incorrect because this is the first step drivers take when completing a look. Choice *B* is incorrect because drivers may receive a failing exam score if they do not maintain three points of contact with the vehicle while vacating. Choice *D* is incorrect because drivers maintain a firm grip on the handrails to steady themselves while leaving the vehicle.

99. D: Choice *D* is correct because drivers stop three feet from the back of the alley in an Alley Dock exercise.

100. A: Choice *A* is correct because drivers complete the Offset Backing exercise by bringing the front of the vehicle behind the first set of cones. Choice *B* is incorrect because the Offset Backing exercise is not complete until after drivers bring the vehicle behind the first set of cones, even though drivers must first bring the vehicle into the opposite lane of traffic. Choice *C* is incorrect because bringing the vehicle out of the way of traffic is a concern for Parallel Parking exercises, rather than a concern for Offset Backing exercises. Choice *D* is correct because this is the criteria for completing the Alley Docking exercise.

Greetings!

First, we would like to give a huge "thank you" for choosing us and this study guide for your CDL exam. We hope that it will lead you to success on this exam and for your years to come.

Our team has tried to make your preparations as thorough as possible by covering all of the topics you should be expected to know. In addition, our writers attempted to create practice questions identical to what you will see on the day of your actual test. We have also included many test-taking strategies to help you learn the material, maintain the knowledge, and take the test with confidence.

We strive for excellence in our products, and if you have any comments or concerns over the quality of something in this study guide, please send us an email so that we may improve.

As you continue forward in life, we would like to remain alongside you with other books and study guides in our library. We are continually producing and updating study guides in several different subjects. If you are looking for something in particular, all of our products are available on Amazon. You may also send us an email!

Sincerely,
APEX Test Prep
info@apexprep.com

FREE

Free Study Tips Videos/DVD

In addition to this guide, we have created a FREE set of videos with helpful study tips. **These FREE videos provide you with top-notch tips to conquer your exam and reach your goals.**

Our simple request is that you give us feedback about the book in exchange for these strategy-packed videos. We would love to hear what you thought about the book, whether positive, negative, or neutral. It is our #1 goal to provide you with quality products and customer service.

To receive your **FREE Study Tips Videos**, scan the QR code or email freevideos@apexprep.com. Please put "FREE Videos" in the subject line and include the following in the email:

   a. The title of the book

   b. Your rating of the book on a scale of 1-5, with 5 being the highest score

   c. Any thoughts or feedback about the book

Thank you!

www.ingramcontent.com/pod-product-compliance
Lightning Source LLC
Chambersburg PA
CBHW060514300426
44112CB00017B/2660